The Emptied Soul

On the Nature of the Psychopath

19

THE EMPTIED SOUL

On the Nature of the Psychopath
(formerly published as *Eros on Crutches*)

ADOLF GUGGENBÜHL-CRAIG

Translated from the German by
Gary V. Hartman

Spring Publications, Inc.
Woodstock, Connecticut

Classics in Archetypal Psychology 1

This book is a translation of *Seelenwüsten—Betrachtungen über Eros und Pychopathie*, published by Raben Reihe, Schweizer Spiegel Verlag, Zürich. The first and second printing of the Spring Publications edition bore the title *Eros on Crutches* and with the subtitle *Reflections on Psychopathy and Amorality* on the first printing.

Published by
Spring Publications, Inc.
299 East Quassett Road;
Woodstock, Connecticut 06281

Printed in Canada.

New edition composed by B. Spalding Harris.
Book designed and edited by JFL.

Library of Congress Cataloging-in-Publication Data

Pending

Contents

FOREWORD

In Roman Catholic mythology, there exists a figure which has always moved me; namely the child in limbo, the unbaptised child who can neither go to Heaven, nor to Hell, nor to Purgatory. This child wanders back and forth in all eternity between Heaven and Hell. Since it is not baptised it cannot go to heaven, and having died at birth, it had no opportunity to sin, so it cannot go to Hell. The figure of the child in limbo was, even for conservative Catholics, too much to swallow, and it has therefore been omitted from most Catholic churches. And yet the following book deals with the part of our psyche which could be represented by the unbaptized child in limbo; unbaptized meaning that part of our psyche which has not been touched by the essence of human nature—by erotic, moral, and aesthetic differentiation.

After I write my books, I usually receive some echo from the public. Often I am informed by readers that a particular book has helped them either to understand themselves better, or helped them in their marriage, or has been of some help to social workers, to therapists, or to whomever. But after publishing *The Emptied Soul*, nothing like that happened. No reviews appeared, and the only comments I got were: "Your book helped me to see my *partner* better, to recognise what a hopeless person he or she is." No one ever seemed to apply the content of the book to him or herself.

My concerns in *The Emptied Soul* are not "in" today. They are not even politically correct—or psychologically correct. Today it is correct to say that we are all born with a psyche which contains every possibility that exists. All the faculties are there—except if there is a genetic defect or a birth injury which, of course, diminishes the psychological possibilities of the psyche. If, in the course of a life history, some empty psychological space appears, it is only because the faculties could not develop due to adverse circumstances like nasty parents, bad environment, and so on. But to have the impudence to point out an empty space in our own soul; even to claim that there may be human beings who have a deficient eros or no eros at all, and that these people may even be socially well adapted, is just too much to accept.

Eros, in the meaning of love altogether—not only sexual love—is usually associated with gentleness, niceness, goodness, kindness, charity, etc. The more eros somebody has, the more likable and charming he or she is—that is the prevailing opinion. That often the opposite can be true, that a person lacking eros can be charming, and that the presence of eros makes life difficult for people, is less well known. Eros means caring, and if someone cares for whatever or whoever it may be, worries, nervousness, even neurotic tensions can be the result. Loving persons are seldom cool and relaxed, but people suffering from a deficient eros are unconcerned and so do not worry; often they are very relaxed and easy going. It is agreeable to be with people who are deficient in eros; they usually know how to behave pleasantly and can be socially delightful—except when eros is needed.

Perhaps a man or a woman started a marriage with a pleasant and delightful partner—a partner who was good fun to be with. But then, as the years went by, the children came into adolescence, started to be difficult, even obstreperous, and maybe financial problems appeared or one partner's job might have been threatened; then the atmosphere changes. At this point eros is required, and just to be a relaxed and charming person is no help. Suddenly the charming, friendly partner who has a weak ego takes off, distances his or herself—it is all too much as now a strong eros is required. "I don't know what happened," friends or neighbours of a couple may say. "He or she was always so charming," not realising that the charm was due to a deficient eros. A truly erotic person, in the sense of a loving person, might be difficult, tense, and even neurotic; a person lacking in eros can be very relaxed, pleasant, nice, and sexually uncomplicated. Eros makes life more difficult; lack of eros can make life easier.

But how about this empty space in our soul? How can anyone be interested in an empty space in our soul? How can anyone be concerned with a vacuum? Nature has a "horror *vaccui*;" we, as part of nature, always shy away from any vacuum. However that may be, I think the existing deficiencies in our soul, even the empty spaces, are important for psychology. It is important that we see them in our fellow human beings and react accordingly to avoid being fooled by the charm, not denying them, but taking them into account. But it is even more important to see these empty spaces in ourselves and not fool ourselves by denying them.

Many of the empty or half-empty spaces in our psyche do not have especially tragic consequences. It does not matter if somebody has a musical *lacuna* or cannot appreciate good food and wine or has no sense of style. But the closer our empty spaces come to eros, the more tragic the situation becomes. It is here that even collectively the most dreadful things happen. For instance the International Classification of Diseases, internationally the more recognised diagnostic psychiatric manual, never mentions eros, nor morals, nor decency. So what does this mean concerning present day psychiatry or psychology?

There is one comforting thought: oddly enough even people with many psychological *lacunae* may they be erotic, moral, etc., have religious longings. Despite the easy-going charm of many people who have a lack of eros, their lives have a tragic quality, a background sadness characterises them because they feel they lack something which although it complicates life, at the same time gives meaning to it. As a result they yearn for redemption; to be rescued from their own emptiness.

Michael Fordham (1995), a famous British analytical psychologist, said analysis ends when one has reached the pathological core of the psyche. I would phrase it differently: no analysis is finished until we clearly recognise our empty or at least half-empty spaces; our inner deserts. And this applies even more to the endeavours of everyone to know himself and herself, because most of the search to recognise and see oneself and others, to become conscious, happens with people who have never heard of analysis. They are the ones for whom I am writing.

Adolf Guggenbühl-Craig
Zürich

CHAPTER ONE
Total Health and the Unhealed Daimon

During the last century and a half, the vanguard of medical science has experienced one triumph after another. Disease, its fiendish adversary, twists and turns, writhing under the blows of the healers' swords, attempting to avoid total eradication. On the other hand doctors are busier than ever. Medical costs are rocketing to astronomical heights with expenditures approaching fifty percent of the national budget. Each new technique, each new machine demands more money: weapons are expensive, and wars are costly undertakings. "What does that matter?" we ask. "The important thing is to win!" We wait with baited breath for the long-promised victory.

The war against disease is not going quite as well as we would like to think. On the contrary a large portion of medical costs has nothing to do with epic struggles which lead to glorious victories. Gone is the day of the great generals—Pasteur, Ehrlich, and Lister. More and more the battles resemble hit-and-run style guerrilla encounters with an elusive, insidious enemy, appearing maddeningly where least expected. Statistics show that thirty to sixty percent of all medical endeavors are concerned with psychosomatic and neurotic disorders. Patients consult their doctors for all sorts of plausible and

1

implausible complaints: backaches, headaches, abdominal pressure, vague sensations of discomfort, fatigue, insomnia, loss of appetite, overeating, skin troubles. This list does not even include the innumerable neurotic afflictions such as compulsions, obsessions, depressions, anxiety, sexual disturbances, crippling complexes and the like. These chronic, psychosomatic, neurotic disturbances are the time-consuming work for physicians, psychiatrists, and psychotherapists. There are two reasons for this phenomenon: first, so many patients suffer from these disorders, and second, they are difficult, if not impossible to heal. Often they follow a seesaw pattern, improving only to get worse. One day the doctor feels to have the thing under control only to be confronted the next day by a patient with the same pain, rash, or fatigue.

For the healers, for doctors and psychotherapists, the struggle often seems like shadowboxing. They employ every method, both medical and psychotherapeutic, at their disposal, sparing neither time nor money, yet seldom experiencing successful breakthroughs. Here is an example of what I mean. A woman was referred to me after having been treated for multiple sclerosis for eight years. The diagnosis proved to be false. I treated her in psychotherapy for another five years. Even though she was cooperative, her fatigue, generalized weakness, and passivity remain today much as they were thirteen years ago.

While all of us as therapists would like to heal, do we ever stop and ask ourselves what it means to heal? The World Health Organization defines "health" as unim-

paired mental, physical, and social well-being and functioning. We have a long way to go before even half of
the human race reaches this condition. In the meantime
a large number of therapists will either lose their initial
optimism and succumb to depression or cynicism, or they
will talk themselves into believing that they have been
more successful than they actually have been.

Clearly, then, there are definite limits to healing, although
the word itself suggests otherwise. "Heal" is related to the
German word, *Heil*, meaning "heal" or "whole." In northern
German dialect the word *Heil* is used in the sense of "whole."
The Swedish word *hel*, "whole," and the Slavic word *celyj*,
"whole" or "complete," belong to the same word family. In
other words when we set about to "heal" our patients,
we want them to become "whole." We would like them
to fulfill their potential in every sense of the word.
But millions, particularly neurotic and psychosomatic
patients, are never really healed. We cannot make them
or help them to become "whole." Despite all of our
efforts, despite preventative medicine, special diets,
physical exercise, gymnastics, jogging, and an almost
endless list of activities, many patients will not become
"whole." Our efforts do not stop there. Since our notion
of health also implies psychological health, we try all
kinds of psychotherapies: individual and group, Trans-
actional Analysis and Transcendental Meditation, yoga
and t'ai chi. Our therapeutic ambitions are bound-
less. However our successes are limited. Is our optimistic
goal of health in the sense of the World Health
Organization's definition as illusory as it is grandiose?

Let us take a case in point and get down to "cases"—
that being the time honored medical and psychoanalytic
approach. Some months ago I read the letters of Jane Carlisle,
the wife of the famous Scottish historian and philosopher, Thomas Carlisle. Apparently she was always ill.
She had continual headaches and backaches, and she
was always catching or recovering from a cold. As she
became older she even took morphine. She is best known
for her witty and interesting letters which leave the impression of such continual and chronic suffering that the
woman must have been an invalid. On the other hand
she traveled extensively and enjoyed an active social
life. Also she was an ambitious woman, delighting in
her husband's renown and supporting his ambitions.
Somehow one is left with the feeling that Mrs. Carlisle
took pleasure in describing her various and sundry
ailments, her pains, her chills, her fevers; and that visi-
tors who came to consult her husband usually concluded
their stay in Lady Carlisle's chambers enquiring after the
state of her health. Although she expected those around
her to attend to and to help alleviate her chronic suffering, it is clear that she did not expect to be healed. She
appears to have viewed her endless disturbances as
part of her life, an integral part of her existence. She
seems to have cultivated the image of chronic illness
and invalidism.

Today we would describe her as a hypochondriac or even
a hysteric, as a highly neurotic woman and a bit of a drug
addict to boot. "Get thee to a therapist" would be our
advice, hoping that someone, the internist, psychotherapist,

or the analyst could, once and for all, relieve her of her suffering. If she had been on welfare, we would have suggested a day clinic or a social worker. There are many people like Jane Carlisle, with one major difference: their illness, their ailments are "not okay." We feel that we must be involved in healing them. Not only the fact that they are ill plagues us. They are often egotistical and tyrannical. Another woman, a Mrs. K., is an example of what I am talking about. Between the ages of thirty and sixty she lived in a small town where the local doctor diagnosed her for all sorts of diseases and disorders: heart trouble, kidney trouble, back and stomach pains. Her case history read like a diagnostic textbook. Despite the countless diagnoses and corresponding treatments, she would not be cured. Her family suffered as much as she did. Her children felt continually guilty. Whenever a family argument started to heat up or an outright confrontation with their mother became inevitable, they were always told, "Mommy doesn't feel well, she needs to have it quiet. You know Mommy is ill." They were made to feel that Mommy was ill because they were such inconsiderate and unloving children. If the children felt guilty, the husband, by contrast, was enslaved. It was his lot to perform any and all unpleasant chores around the house because his wife "didn't feel very well," and the doctor had said, "She needs her rest." She not only tyrannized her family, she also developed a missionary zeal for illness: one of her daughters—healthy though she was—was declared a "sickly child," and everyone including the girl believed it.

What is it that is going on with Mrs. Carlisle, Mrs. K., and millions of similar cases? What is it that thwarts our well-meaning efforts at healing? What is this seemingly inhuman element which defies the best intentions of doctor, patient, and therapist? It would appear to be some force, some power, an invincible demon, or perhaps, *daimon*. It is a *daimon* that we repeatedly attempt to get hold of, to destroy, or at least to neutralize with theories and explanations, only to find it slipping through our fingers or mercurially assuming another guise. The forms which psychosomatic and neurotic disorders assume change. This is a historical fact. People do not fall into a dead faint as frequently as they did eighty years ago; women no longer suffer from "vapors," and girls no longer are diagnosed "anemic." Instead we have anorexia, allergies, and dermatitis. In spite of all our efforts, we are no more in control of this *daimon* of invalidism now than we have been in the past.

CHAPTER TWO
The Archetype of the Invalid

Let us come back to the question of the nature of this force or forces, this *daimon,* which defies our well-intentioned attempts at total health. Might we not be dealing with an archetype? The question is not so farfetched. It is one which we must pose whenever we are confronted with a psychological phenomenon which cannot be rationally or logically explained or understood. Here I understand "archetype" not so much as an image but rather as "an inborn pattern of behavior in a classical, typically human situation." This agrees with C. G. Jung's later works.

Invalidism has certainly always been with us. All living things, all human beings, come into this world deficient, lacking in something, whether it be due to heredity, prenatal infection, or birth trauma. We become more and more deficient as our lives progress: accidents, illnesses, and the aging process itself leave permanent damages. The older we are, the greater our degree of invalidism. In some manner or other, all of our physical, mental, and psychic functions are impaired. Having to live with and react to such deficiencies is a typically human situation. Therefore since we spoke above of an archetype as a reaction to a "typically human situation," could we not conclude that invalidism is archetypal in nature?

These deficiencies may affect us to a greater or lesser degree. We might not even think twice about being color-blind or having one leg slightly shorter than the other, while mental retardation or debility would be much more serious. Loss of sight in one eye would not markedly interfere with the potential for our development; total deafness due to an explosion, on the other hand, is another matter. Being overly excitable following a brain concussion does not have the same effect upon our lives as the personality changes that accompany various diseases of the brain and nervous system. (Since the brain holds a central place in our psychic and emotional functioning, we find the greatest spectrum of invalidism in connection with this organ.) Because the confrontation with deficiencies, with invalidism, plays such an important role in human life, we might be justified in speaking of an "archetypal" reaction. For the purpose of discussion, then, let us assume that there is an Archetype of the Invalid. Let us assume that the *daimon* at work in our chronic state of deficiency is the Archetype of the Invalid.

Before going on, I should like to make some general remarks on the nature of archetypes. No one knows how archetypes came to be or in what form they first appeared. Jung assumed that they were a reaction to recurring situations. For the purposes of our discussion, the "how" is not as important as the fact that an archetype was initially a reaction to a particular, concrete experience. With the passage of time, however, the archetype became separated from the experience itself, assuming a degree of autonomy. In other words archetypes can and do manifest themselves without the concrete, external situation. The Mother Archetype, for example, can be lived out by a woman, whether she has children or not. It affects and colors her experience of herself and the world around her. It is possible, for instance, that the concept of a "permissive society" is an expression of the Mother Archetype. "Mother" allows all, forgives all, not only in connection with children. We often speak of a "patriarchal" society or of "patriarchal" values. "Patriarchal" implies the rule of the Father. But this fatherliness does not refer to children, to the biological act of procreation, but rather to the structuring of our society, a society in which the archetype of the father is dominant. While the pattern may have originated in the experience of a father's relationship to his children, it now includes the behavior of an entire society.

We find the autonomy of the archetype over and against external situations in the case of the Archetype of the Invalid. Therefore it might manifest itself whether the person in question is an invalid or not. Generally a person who has lost an eye or a leg lives out to a greater or lesser degree the Archetype of the Invalid. This is not always the case and frequently not to the extent we might expect. On the other hand someone with no apparent disability may behave as if they were an invalid. The actual state of invalidism has little or no effect on how one experiences life.

If the Invalid is to be seen as an archetypal phenomenon, so must Health, i.e., the fantasy of total health as the World Health Organization defines it. Both perspectives provide a way of viewing our experience of ourselves and our world. Although neither is right or wrong, the portrayal of Health in this book may seem one-sided since I am looking at it from the perspective of the invalid. Either perspective can be harmful, particularly when it is exclusively one-sided. The disciples of Health, with a capital "H"—*mens sana in corpore sano*—worship health, viewing themselves only as healthy, no matter how sickly or disabled they might be. They go jogging three months after a coronary. Although perhaps diabetic, they might undertake long and arduous wilderness treks. They return to full-time work following major surgery. They eat the proper foods, see an analyst if they have problems, and consult marriage counselors if they cannot understand their spouses. They radiate health right up until the day they die— "He wasn't sick a day of his life." They are octogenarian members of a Matterhorn expedition. They regale one and all with stories about their health, completely overlooking the fact that no one—repeat, no one—can be that healthy. We are all born invalids. None of us is perfect, even though our deficiency might be as insignificant as a slight lack of coordination, or that we are a bit under or overweight, or that we hunch our shoulders.

Health and invalidism seem to be opposing ways of viewing life. One can either see oneself as healthy, strong, and "whole," or as deficient, lacking somehow in body and psyche. From the health perspective deficiencies, disabilities, and *lacunae* are but temporary problems which must

10

be overcome; from the invalid's perspective they are simply part of life.

If there is an Archetype of the Invalid, should there not be a mythological personification of it? Do not archetypes usually appear in mythology as gods or goddesses? Were not such representations the basis for Jung's theory of archetypes? Where then, in which mythologies, do we find the invalid as a collective image?

The Greek gods seem to be anything but invalids. In keeping with their exalted position, they are portrayed as perfect beings. There are only two exceptions: Hephaistos, who limps, and Achilles with his vulnerable heel. Even the perfect hero has a weakness.

Moving to Germanic mythology we find a different state of affairs. Here there are numerous examples of invalids. In fact the whole of Germanic mythology seems to be overshadowed by an atmosphere of foreboding—the Nidhoggr gnawing at the roots of Yggdrasil, the World Tree, and the knowledge of the impending *Goetterdaemerung*. We find Thor, the god of war, with a mill stone embedded in his forehead—a painful memento of an early battle. Other Germanic gods suffer from severe wounds, are missing a hand or something of the sort. Baldur, the shining one, is invincible against anything except the parasitic mistletoe. Invalidism seems to be of greater importance for Germanic mythology than it was for the Greeks.

Many mythologies—the Mexican and Hindu—often portray their gods as grotesque beings. Similarly we find bizarre deities from prehistoric cultures which give a crippled impression.

Artists often create mythological images of this kind. I see the paintings of Velasquez, for instance, as an expression of the Archetype of the Invalid. His figures are frequently grotesque and distorted. The filmmaker Fellini flavors his works heavily with invalids—the crippled, perverse, and abnormal aspects of the human race, the elephantine woman or skeletal man. The invalid as a mythical image and symbol appears also in classical adventure stores. One is reminded of the pirate stories, of Long John Silver with his peg leg in Robert Louis Stevenson's *Treasure Island*, or Peter Pan's archrival, Captain Hook with his metallic prosthesis. The figure of the pirate, in itself an image of the invalid, traditionally is missing an arm or leg or at least has a patch over one eye. Another familiar image of the invalid from literature is Victor Hugo's Quasimodo, the Hunchback of Notre Dame. In general the arts seem to point to the Archetype of the Invalid—what are the gargoyles on the Cathedral of Notre Dame, if not invalids?

Given the Archetype of the Invalid, there must also be an invalid complex since archetypes draw parts of the psyche and psychic experience to themselves. This is what is meant by a complex. A man who has a father complex tends to experience life within the framework of the patriarchal, whether it has to do with "father" and "fathering" or not. A policeman, for example, makes him feel like a small boy being confronted by his paternal parent. There is, in point of fact, an invalid complex. In the course of my work as a psychotherapist, I have often encountered women—and men as

12

well—who could only fall in love with invalids. They were sexually attracted only to those who were physical invalids.

Allow me to sketch out a brief "differential diagnosis" of the Archetype of the Invalid by way of definition and comparison. The invalid must not be confused with the archetype of the child. The child, like the invalid, is weak and inferior, lacking the qualities of the adult. The child, however, grows, changes, becomes adult, "kills the father." It has a future. The Archetype of the Invalid must also not be confused with that of illness. Illness, much like the child, has a future. It leads to death, to health or, even, to invalidism. It is temporal, a passing threat, a catastrophe. Illness may well impair psychic or physical functioning, but it is acute, dynamic, temporary. Invalidism leads nowhere, neither to death nor to health. Ultimately it is chronic, a lasting deficiency. It is a chronic state of being "out of order."

Those who live out the Archetype of the Invalid can be tiresome and annoying to those around them. I might note parenthetically that only one other archetype makes people so tiresome and annoying: the archetype or the fantasy of health. A person who goes on and on about his bad back is pretty boring but is nothing compared to someone who never tires of telling about his physical prowess, how his heart still beats regularly and rhythmically after jogging six miles, how he gets up every morning at six o'clock to take an ice-cold shower.

Of course an archetype in and of itself is neither good nor bad, neither interesting nor boring. Depending on the situation and our point of view, it can seem to be negative or positive. Our job as psychotherapists is to study and reflect on the archetypes and their characteristics, to allow ourselves to be amazed by them, to learn, in some small measure, to deal with them in actual experience. The Archetype of the Invalid can be annoying; it can, on the other hand, be very pleasant, as in the following example.

I knew a middle-aged man who suffered from chronic back pains, periodic depressions, and continual fatigue. At the same time, he was a nice person to have around—he made others feel helpful and useful. You could always do something for him like finding him a comfortable arm chair. He seemed to appreciate gestures of this sort. He was in no way a threat to those around him; there was no sense of competitiveness for their time and attention. He made you feel kindly and generous, provoking a friendly, accepting attitude in others. It was most relaxing to be with him. If the Archetype of the Invalid is recognized and respected, it gives rise to reflection and discussion. In the case of this man, whenever someone would suggest going for a walk, he would reply, "No, thank you, my back hurts. Why don't we stay here and chat a little?"

The Archetype of the Invalid can be fruitful for the person living it out. It counteracts inflation; it cultivates modesty. Because human weakness and failings are given their due, a kind of spiritualization is possible. Invalidism is a continual *memento mori,* an on-going confrontation with physical and psychic limitations. It allows no escape into fantasies of health or away from an awareness of death. It

14

promotes patience and curbs obsessional doing. In a way it is a very *human* archetype. The fantasy of health and wholeness in body and soul may be suitable for the gods, but for mere mortals it is a tribulation. *Quod licet jovi non licet bovi.*

Because the Archetype of the Invalid emphasizes human dependence, because it forces acceptance of our mutual need of and for others, it is an important factor in relationships. We are haunted today by a psychological *fata morgana*—the illusion of the Independent Person. There are still those who believe it possible to be totally independent of others. *All* of us are dependent on someone—on husbands or wives, on fathers or mothers, on our children, friends, even our neighbors. Knowledge of our own deficiencies and weaknesses, of our own invalidism, helps us to realize our eternal dependence on someone or something. A person who is a "cripple" in regard to feelings will always be dependent on those with a "healthy" feeling life. Mutual, as well as one-sided dependency, comes into its own with the Archetype of the Invalid. It serves as a counterbalance to the "rolling stone gathers no moss" image of the wandering hero, a popular figure among members of the younger generation. For them the ideal is to move like free spirits throughout the world with no attachments, no hindrances: today in India and tomorrow in Mexico. Freedom and independence are their alpha and omega, the be-all-and-end-all of their existence.

Another area in which the Archetype of the Invalid plays an important role is the phenomenon of transference in psychotherapy. Dependency in psychotherapy is generally understood as a father or mother transference and is viewed as a regression. Unfortunately the child/ parent regression fantasy in psychotherapy can be damaging. More often than not a client's dependency reflects not the child but the invalid. Sometimes clients remain dependent on their therapists for years—the child seems never to grow up. How can it? We are not dealing with a *child* but with an invalid and his or her corresponding need to be dependent! In these situations the analyst often develops a guilty conscience. The analyst asks if one is not, perhaps unconsciously, trying to maintain a full practice by constellating the analysand's dependency. The question is out of place. The analyst is not being unethical but is serving in a legitimate fashion as the invalid's crutch. Although the analyst might attempt to shift the analysand's need for dependency to someone else, to a neighbor or a friend, one thing is certain: the crutch will always be necessary. The goal of total independence is simply unrealistic. If, on the other hand, the analyst identifies with the fantasy of health, of wholeness, and growth, the analyst simply will not see what is happening. The analyst believes to be dealing with the child archetype. One fails to realize that the absence of growth and healing points to the invalid, not to the child. The child, as we noted above, grows and requires help only for a time.

I must reiterate that the difficulties and attendant dangers in dealing with the invalid can never be overestimated. It is just these difficulties and dangers which frequently result in both a collective and individual repression, characterized by the slogan, "The invalid shall always be with us!" In our confrontation with invalidism, we all too readily succumb to a fatalistic attitude, to passivity that says, "Why bother? There is nothing we can do anyway!" Lacking the proper understanding of the Archetype of the Invalid, we give up, we stop trying to heal that which can be healed. To some extent the great strides made in both medicine and psychiatry are a result of the repression of the invalid. We have become so captivated by the fantasy of total health that we are indefatigable in our efforts towards its realization. Yet we analysts should not be the first to cast stones: the fantasy of health fills our practices just as surely as does that of invalidism.

If I appear *ipso facto* as a self-appointed attorney for the defense in the case "health vs. invalidism," it is because the Archetype of the Invalid has too long been ignored; it has not been granted the respect it deserves. My attacks on "health," the prosecution's position, are not intended to discredit but rather to help achieve some semblance of balance between essential perspectives. To further develop my case, I should like to point out the pitfalls of the health/wholeness archetype, my worthy opponent.

According to the contemporary fantasy of health, we must become whole where wholeness is understood in the sense of perfection: "Be ye perfect . . ." The slightest defect, the least malfunction must be cured, removed, or eradicated. Although there was a time when a melancholic temperament was accepted, even idealized, today melancholies are diagnosed as "depressive," are tranquil-ized and medicated to the point of being blissful vegetables. Deep down inside we are all aware of our failings, our weakness, our invalidism. At the same time we repress this realization by whatever means possible. We struggle endlessly, senselessly, to maintain the illusion of wholeness by trying to achieve perfect health.

Our blindness to the place and importance of the invalid archetype becomes a moralistic attitude, holding health and wholeness as the ultimate good. It is not hard to imagine how devastating this attitude is in dealing with those suffering from neuroses and psychosomatic disorders. I am continually struck by the tone of moral superiority that creeps into psychotherapists' voices when discussing cases of this nature. Neurotics and psychosomatics are simply inferior; they cannot be healed because they do not want to be. They do not want to change; they do not want to grow. They refuse our attempts for their betterment. They will not even listen to their dreams! Like drowning people, they cling to their resistances, defending themselves, as we see it, tenaciously against the therapist who is only trying to help them. Such people, such poor, benighted souls are only worthy of our attention when they embrace our growth/health/wholeness fantasy (is it a fantasy or is it a delusional fixation?). As therapists we are only inter-ested in them when they *want* to be healed.

I do not wish to leave the impression that all patients are chronic cases or cannot be healed. I merely wish to point out that, in instances where the Archetype of the Invalid is manifested, healing and wholeness are simply not possible. To accept this fact might seem immoral, both to patient and analyst. However the positive effects will soon offset any lingering doubts. Because healing and wholeness are so much in vogue these days, we desperately need to reflect on and accept the invalid archetype.

To ignore or denigrate an archetype invites its wrath and vengeance, and the Archetype of the Invalid is no exception. It seems that the harder we try to heal chronic neurotic or psychosomatic patients, the more desperately they resist. They become more tyrannical, more demanding, and claim more of our time and attention. Far from healing, our efforts seem but to exacerbate the condition. It would appear that many people are simply waiting for the moment when they can openly claim their invalidism. A minor accident, a slight decrease of some physical or mental capacity, and they give up their jobs, claim disability insurance, and expect that others will take care of them. In each of us they arouse guilt feelings. They seem to say, "Now I'm an invalid. Now it is up to you to take care of me." It is our failure to accept the invalid in each of us, our fantasy that human beings should be as healthy as those idealized Greek gods, that makes us unable to cope with the Archetype of the Invalid when we meet it. Our guilt forces us to pay homage to what we refuse to accept.

While weakness appears in conjunction with invalidism, it is by no means synonymous, an aspect which is all too often overlooked. Jane Carlisle, of whom I spoke earlier, was extremely capable. She was able to benefit through her own efforts from her husband's fame. She traveled, attended countless parties, and enjoyed an active and intensive social life. Another example is one of my patients. The woman was extremely neurotic, suffering from all kinds of psychosomatic disorders. She had difficulty sleeping, she woke at the slightest sound. She had allergic rashes, suffered every summer from nasal congestion, could only eat specially prepared food, and could tolerate only certain kinds of bed sheets. She had a panicky fear of insects, anxiety about infectious diseases drove her to despair, and the slightest draft was pure torture. This "wreck" of a woman undertook expeditions to the most primitive and unexplored areas of Southeast Asia. She must have had to sleep in incredibly filthy and dangerous conditions, where insects abounded, where even to move in one's sleep was to invite the sting of a scorpion or the bite of a spider. In spite of her continual neurotic and psychosomatic symptoms, this woman ventured into areas where most "normal" mortals would never have dared to tread.

In this connection I would like to mention the concept of compensation as Alfred Adler used it. Initially one of Freud's pupils who later established his own psychology, Adler stated that human beings compensate for so-called organ inferiority. Adler is particularly interesting within the framework of this discussion because of his fascination with the Archetype of the Invalid. He saw neurotic development as a direct reaction to feelings of inferiority arising from actual, physical disabilities. In other words, he viewed human behavior from the perspective of the invalid. In his writings we find detailed descriptions of the various forms which the Archetype of the Invalid assumes. He reduced the whole of human psychology to reactions to ever-present physical weaknesses.

Many of our patients are clearly invalids. In order to provide them with the help they need—since healing is not possible—we must bring them to the point where they can live with their deficiency. In therapy we have to work *with* the Archetype of the Invalid, helping our patients to see that their process of individuation includes their invalidism. To work without it, to exclude it, would be but an illusion. Let me explain what I mean.

Human beings operate out of four basic modes or functions: thinking, feeling, sensation, and intuition. Theoretically we all have at least the potential of all four: one function is superior, another is inferior, and the remaining two are auxiliary. The High Priests of Health and Wholeness would have us help our patients to develop all four. However many patients, for some reason or other, lack one or two of these functions. It is as if they were deformed or crippled. For example if they are missing the feeling function, it would be pointless to help them to develop what is not there. We would, rather, do better to help them explore the measure of their deficiency, show them how to live with it, and demonstrate how a relationship with someone who, for example, had a well-developed feeling function. Attempting to develop all four functions with such patients would only lead to disappointment and frustration for both patient and therapist. Instead of accepting and respecting the patient as is—an invalid—there is the danger that therapist and patient will not only reject invalidism but will also despise it. The result for the patient can understandably be disastrous. Are not we analysts really the advocates of the Archetype of the Invalid? Is not that what we should be about?

The psyche is viewed on one hand as being archetypal, functioning according to given, universal patterns of behavior and experience. On the other hand, it demonstrates completely individual, unique characteristics. The images of wholeness and invalidism are both universals—in other words, archetypal. Let us ask ourselves whether they are two, totally different archetypes or whether they belong together as aspects of the same archetype. The image of invalidism cannot exist without the image of wholeness; the figure of the Imperfect can only be seen upon the ground of the Perfect.

For purposes of discussion, it is easier to speak of two separate archetypes. However, in the final analysis, both Wholeness and Invalidism are aspects of the Self, representing polarities within our psyche. Unfortunately, when we talk about the Self, there is much too much said about qualities like roundness, completeness, and wholeness. It is high time that we spoke of the deficiency, the invalidism of the Self. I have always had difficulty with the fact that mandalas are regarded as symbols par excellence of the Self—they are much too whole for my taste. People come to the realization of themselves, of their Selves, through their invalidism;

completeness is fulfilled through incompleteness. The process must be delineated, perceived, and experienced. Admittedly, it is difficult to sustain the image of completeness and wholeness, and at the same time, to accept invalidism. Inevitably one or the other will be emphasized. During the Middle Ages until the Reformation, the grotesque and deformed in humanity reigned. Today we have succumbed to the cult of the complete, healthy, and round, culminating in a mandala-like perfection.

CHAPTER THREE
Eros

Those who identify with and live out the Archetype of the Invalid can be either creative or uncreative, pleasant or unpleasant, interesting or boring. The negative aspects of the archetype are often pronounced. I mentioned some of them earlier: tyranny, egoism, self-centeredness, exploitation of others' guilt, escapism. The positive aspects include modesty, the capacity for reflection, acceptance of dependence, and a sense for the religious. All archetypes demonstrate both pleasant and unpleasant, creative and destructive qualities. How an archetype is experienced does not depend on the nature of the archetype. "Well, then," we might ask, "what does it depend on?" In order to answer this question, I would like to say a word about a particular Greek god, Eros.

According to Greek mythology, Eros is the oldest of the gods, although there are some tales which make him the youngest. Whether oldest or youngest, it is clear that he is a special god different from the others. He is the god of love. Here love is understood to include the entire spectrum of emotional attachment, from sexuality and friendship to involvement with profession, hobbies, and art. Eros is at work in the love which men have for women and women for men. Eros is also present in politicians whose "love" is politics, or in mathematicians whose passion is mathematics, or in flower fanciers who live for their roses. It is to Eros' credit that gods and goddesses, gods and mortals, come together as lovers so that new gods and demigods are born. Without him there would be no movement among the gods; in fact there would be no gods at all. It is Eros who makes the gods—the archetypes—loving, creative, and involved. Only through Eros can gods or archetypes be loving. As far as we mortals are concerned, gods are neutral, inhuman, distanced, and cold. Only when they are combined with Eros do we sense their movement, do they become creative, intimate, and stimulating.

Here are some examples of what I am talking about. The warrior without Eros is a brutal mercenary, a senseless mass murderer, a demonic exterminator. With Eros the warrior fights to defend values which are important for him. He is ready to lay down his life for others or for higher ideals. A trickster without Eros is but a common cheat and liar, an imposter, a confidence artist. With Eros the trickster is surprising, stimulating, not bogged down in convention and routine but continually revealing new sides of himself and opening unexpected vistas to those around him. He is playful and charming. The Mother Archetype without Eros is overprotective, smothering her children in material security, concerned only with food, warmth, and safety. Children are but tools to be used for personal aggrandizement, a selfish extension of the mother herself. With Eros, however, the child, loved for its own sake, is inculcated with ideals, values, and visions. The role of the mother becomes not merely one of biological propagation, but also one of passing on and nurturing the spirit of humanity.

The Archetype of the Invalid is no different than any other archetype. With Eros the invalid evokes helpfulness and a friendly openness. Invalids can be modest, unheroic, and lead one to philosophical and religious contemplation. They do not get caught up in the power games of competition but recognize the limitations of the human body and *psyche*. Their melancholy is creative. Invalids without Eros are nasty, tyrannical, boring, and parasitic. They compensate for their invalidity by dominating others. They are spoilsports, infantile, pessimistic, filled with hate for themselves and others. Whether the incarnation of the Archetype of the Invalid be a blessing or a curse depends upon Eros. How an archetype, any archetype, is experienced depends upon Eros' presence or absence.

Let there be no mistake: Eros is no savior; he is not the key to living "happily ever after." While Eros makes the archetypes more human, tempering their demonic qualities, he himself can be quite demonic. Much of life's tragedy and comedy, sadness and joy, despair and jubilation arise out of the conflicts and confusion which Eros evokes. To be in love with someone or something leads to suffering, conflict, problems, and frustrations, but also to joy and satisfaction.

The Eros archetype raises some important considerations. Until now little has been written about the relationship among archetypes. To be sure individual archetypes have been discussed and described, but not how one or more archetypes influence the others. At the same time it is just this mutual influence, this relationship, which plays such a decisive role in understanding human behavior. The presence or absence of relationship among archetypes in an individual is the determining factor for character and fate. This relationship depends on Eros, as I will discuss later.

CHAPTER FOUR
Outsiders, Delinquents, and Invalids of Eros (Psychopaths)

I have spoken about invalids in the widest sense of the word, suggesting the concept of the Archetype of the Invalid and exploring various manifestations of it. We usually conceive of invalidism as a physical condition, but there are also psychic invalids as well. Invalidism can be minor, a peripheral phenomenon, or it can assume a central position in an individual's life. One instance of a central invalidism is what has been called psychopathy, a psychiatric diagnosis which is somewhat unfashionable at the moment. It is taken to mean a congenital personality variant which leads to personal and social suffering. Let us examine to what extent psychopathy is related to one of the most basic forms of invalidism, the invalidism of eros. If eros is seen as the factor which makes any archetype—including that of invalidism—creative, human, and positive, what happens when the locus of invalidism is eros itself?

So that the reader may better understand what I am writing about, I want to say something concerning the phenomenology of psychopathy and then go on to discuss its history. Psychopathy is not an "in" diagnosis. The word has become an insult but still finds wide usage among laymen, doctors, psychologists, and teenagers.

Although the term has definite shortcomings, it seems to speak to the fantasy of many and apparently carries certain psychological implications.

"Psychopath," "psychopathy," comes from the Greek *psyche*, soul, and *pathos*, suffering. A psychopath, then, is one whose suffering is of the soul or who is mentally ill. It is no longer used in this sense, now implying immorality, instability, unreliability, and even criminality. Even if we accept the condescending implications of this usage, the diagnosis is frequently misused. The following cases are all of people who were diagnosed psychopaths and will serve as the basis for a more detailed discussion of psychopathy. I hope to demonstrate the importance that the term and the phenomenon of psychopathy still have for us today, for laymen, doctors, and psychologists alike.

The first case is that of a thirty-five year old man who had served six prison sentences. All six times he had been found guilty of theft—theft and not armed robbery. He broke into private homes, stole something, and then sold it. On numerous occasions he had collected welfare under false pretences. While his crimes were not serious, he committed them over and over again. He never lived in one place longer than one or two years despite the fact that he was married and had children. Wherever he went he was disliked. At the time of his last trial he was examined by a psychiatrist who diagnosed him a psychopath. According to the report, he was a man whose personality prevented him from leading an orderly and stable life. The psychiatrist established that he lacked all sense of morality, living by no personal moral code whatsoever. Dependability, respect for property, perseverance, and industry meant nothing to him. He demonstrated a hostility towards and a clear rejection of any kind of social structures or demands. Because of the strained nature of his relationship to society, it might be more applicable to label this man a sociopath, rather than a psychopath. A second psychiatric examination revealed that both diagnoses, sociopath and psychopath, could be misconstrued and were inappropriate.

The man was a member of a subculture somewhat similar to gypsies found in the eastern part of Switzerland, in the Grisons. The psychiatric examination showed that the man possessed a definite moral and social consciousness as far as his own people were concerned. The only trouble was that his group did not identify with the standards of the rest of society. He was a pleasant, congenial sort of fellow and was easy to get to know once you had overcome his initial distrust. He was a poor worker: holding down a job was simply not of any importance in his culture. The first psychiatrist described him as a psychopath or sociopath, because the man could not identify with social norms. As a result either he suffered from society or it from him. However, within his own group, he was anything but asocial. He was respected, well liked, and loyal to friends and acquaintances. Furthermore, he abided strictly by the standards of his own people.

The second case is that of a twenty-two year old girl who, as a ward of the court, had been assigned a guardian. Her guardian was constantly forced to take action against her since she persisted in working as a prostitute. She committed minor thefts, sometimes stealing from her clients. The girl acted embittered, believing that most people disliked her. Even though she was of above-average intelligence, it was difficult to carry on a conversation with her, let alone to get to know her. Her family history was most unhappy: a weak and brutal father, a mother who was never at home. It was the old story of the neglected child whose parents did not love her. Her teachers rejected her and made school a torture. The father blamed the girl's teachers, the school board, and any and all public officials who had anything to do with the family for her difficulties. They were all out to get him and his family. The girl herself was extremely suspicious, refusing suggestions or assistance. According to her case file, this state of affairs had existed since she was twelve years old.

The following story is typical. She quit school after the ninth grade, and a social worker tried to find her an apprenticeship. The girl said she wanted to train as a technical draftsman, and a corresponding position was found. After a couple of weeks, however, the girl quit, saying, "They just stuck me here without asking what I wanted to do." When it came time for her confirmation a year later, her parents could not afford new clothes and shoes for her. Out of sympathy for her plight, a member of the community bought her a pair of shoes with money out of his own pocket, but before the ceremony, the girl picked a fight with her benefactor, angrily accusing him of buying the shoes to make fun of her. She rejected everything that was done for her and was particularly incensed when people tried to help her. The court psychiatrist diagnosed her a psychopath.

Our third "psychopath" was a businessman who, despite his success, had his ups and downs. On several occasions he had been close to bankruptcy only to have Lady Luck smile on him. In time he managed to amass a considerable fortune. When I met him he was in one of his successful phases. I should note that he did not come into therapy of his own accord but was sent by his wife who could hardly stand to live with him any longer.

She described him as superficial, the same impression which I had. Although he was fairly intelligent, he had trouble in school, could not concentrate, and from about the age of thirteen, moved from one school to another. He was not unruly or a troublemaker; he kept moving because his grades were bad. He finally managed to graduate from high school and enrolled in the university. After hanging around there for a couple of years he went to work for his brother, later starting his own business. He was well-liked where he lived, had many acquaintances but few friends. His wife, on the other hand, experienced him as brutal and indifferent. "My husband is a psychopath," she said. "He doesn't love me, he doesn't love anyone! People like him, however, because he's always the life of the party. The only reason he is so successful in his work is because he doesn't mind taking risks. Nothing bothers him. Even when it looks like he is going bankrupt, he still gets a good night's rest. Over and over again he risks all he has without thinking twice about it!" His immediate family, in contrast to his acquaintances, had a decided dislike for him. Although they continually tried to be nice and to relate to him, they were always put off by his indifference and distanced attitude. It was not only his wife who labeled him a psychopath. The psychiatrist whom he consulted at his wife's insistence telephoned me and said, "The poor woman is married to a psychopath!"

The fourth case was that of a thirty-five year old man who was tried for murder. According to him, this was not the first time he had killed someone. He seemed to enjoy making an impression on others by describing how violent he was by nature, and how it did not bother him in the least to kill another human being. His life had been quite turbulent. His mother did not want him, and at the age of three sent him to live with an aunt. He never knew his father. He was always at odds with those around him, and in school he got into one fight after another, often causing bodily harm to his classmates. He had no sense of responsibility, living by the law of the jungle, survival at whatever cost necessary. He could be quite friendly and polite, someone who enjoyed conversation and cocktail party-like discussions, but someone for whom it was difficult to get a feeling as a person. He was labeled a psychopath in the sense of moral debility.

What, then, do these four people have in common? They are all characterized by qualities which lead to difficulty with their environment and to personal suffering.

None of them is mentally ill; none of them has a disturbed relationship with reality. Yet something about them is not in order. For one reason or another their social behavior is different, contrasting with prevailing social norms.

The first case, the man who kept landing in jail, did adhere to social norms, the only problem being that his "society" differed from that of most people. The conflict was not between him and society, but between his society—to whose standards he was extremely loyal— and that of the majority. What created trouble for him was his relationship to property. He did not regard property as something which allows freedom, but as a quantum: some had too much, others had too little. Since he had too little, he felt justified in appropriating some from those who had too much. He was neither aggressive nor destructive. He had definite moral standards, those of his subculture, which were important and binding. The following story exemplifies these standards.

According to his family's tradition, a newborn child was "christened" by the family circle in a rather exotic, barbarous ceremony. Several days later the family would go to the Catholic priest, who christened the child and gave it a present. In like manner the child would then be taken to the Protestant minister for his christening and present. It did not always work, but usually they could find some clergyman who would carry out another ceremony, little guessing that the child had already been baptized two or three times. The important thing was to see how many presents the family could get. As far as they could tell, that was the whole point of the official christening. They did not consider it deceitful or wrong in any way. They were not amoral; they simply had different morals!

A certain amount of tension always occurs whenever two cultures meet, particularly when this confrontation takes place in a specific location. The situation is most difficult for members of the minority culture since they are often despised and rejected, perceived as lacking certain important moral standards. (In recent history the Jews are the best example of this kind of discrimination.) The diagnosis of psychopathy was not justified in this case: the man was completely normal.

The second case is different. The girl came from a family which was openly opposed to prevailing social values and standards. While not belonging to a minority culture, the girl did espouse the values of her immediate social environment. Her relationship to her family was bad; to a certain extent her parents had betrayed her. The brutal father and the absent mother were unable or unwilling to give their daughter what she needed and expected. As the girl grew up, meeting more and more people, she projected the disappointments experienced with her parents onto society as a whole. It was not that she rejected the prevailing social values, but that she regarded the whole thing as a trick, a plot aimed at her. The betrayal experienced at the hands of her parents was transferred in her mind to society. Her antagonistic attitude became even more pronounced as her own negativity—her shadow qualities of destruction and evil—was projected upon representatives of the social structure. Since she experienced her parents and herself as destructive, evil, and antagonistic, society came to personify those qualities which she could not accept in herself. Her parents supported her antisocial attitudes partially to avoid seeing their own betrayal and partially to avoid the hate and rejection of their daughter. They encouraged her to regard society's representatives—teachers, social workers, policemen, and clergy—as the devil himself.

On the other hand the girl was capable of forming relationships, of becoming emotionally intimate with others. It was difficult to get to know her as her initial reaction to strangers was one of enmity. However she was not cool and withdrawn. It was also not difficult to identify with her position. To a certain extent she was moralistic, accusing her environment of not being moral. She repeated again and again that others mistreated her, that she was lied to and cheated. Her standards for herself and those around her were actually quite high. She was loyal to her friends and stood up for acquaintances whom she felt had also been rejected by society. She had a well-developed ethical sense and was capable of love and hate, of emotional and intimate relationships with others.

In this case the diagnosis psychopathy seems out of place if not incorrect. Social neurosis would have been more fitting. Her neurosis was her projection of her negative childhood experiences, as well as her own negative qualities, onto society and its representatives. Essentially the girl's personality was not so different from that of other human beings. While she did not belong to a minority culture like the first man, she did feel excluded and rejected by the culture and society to which she belonged and whose values she shared. We meet this phenomenon fairly frequently. Do not all of us tend to make society and official figures into carriers of projections from our negative childhood experiences and of our own destructive tendencies?

The first social group of any importance for a child is quite small. Generally it consists of the immediate family: parents, siblings, possibly close relatives, widening later to include classmates, playmates, and the neighborhood in which the child lives. Should children experience parents as rejecting, they frequently reject in return without even realizing it. When children enter puberty their relationship with the initial social group, the family, is projected upon society as a whole: society becomes the enemy. Already in the first grade, both the girl and her parents thought the teacher had it in for her. In almost delusional fashion the teacher's behavior was misinterpreted, becoming a self-fulfilling prophecy: because the girl reacted with enmity toward the teacher, he treated her in like manner.

This defiant, rejecting attitude which I have called social neurotic is often found among teenagers and might be confused with a kind of revolutionary attitude. However, revolutionaries, while they may be destructive, destroy in order to clear the way for something new. They are eminently social creatures, despite the fact that the society they propose is not the existing one, but the one which will supplant the present one. True revolutionaries offer alternatives. The girl whose case we have been discussing was not after an alternative social order. Her values, as already stated, were the same as the society by which she felt persecuted. It was a black-and-white issue with the existing society carrying the blackness of her negative projections.

In these two cases, that of the first man and this girl, it would be inappropriate to speak of psychic invalidism or psychopathy. There is nothing wrong with their personalities. They demonstrate all of the basic abilities which one would expect in a so-called "normal" individual, even though their relationship to society was negatively colored by social and familial attitudes. Given the proper circumstances, both are capable of developing satisfactorily. With a little help from her friends, the girl will be able to deal with some of her negative projections. The man discussed in the first case might have occasional difficulty with the law but can live a useful life within his own group, possibly even adjusting to prevailing social norms. In neither case do we see evidence of congenital character variants, of psychic invalidism, of psychopathy.

These two cases represent two categories which are often confused, where the distinctions between them become indistinct. They are, however, basically different. The man's difficulties with society stemmed from an ethnic background; those of the girl from a social neurotic family. The man's problems arose from a cultural difference, while the girl's were attributable to a disturbed development within the culture. In the girl's case the disturbed development was reflected in social attitudes.

The third and fourth cases are another matter. They represent a particular type of human being which, in all likelihood, must be characterized as a psychic invalid. Taking a closer look at them forces us to pose basic questions concerning human nature: what is a human being? What are we born with, and what do we acquire during the course of our lives? In the last two cases something basic seems to be missing. Here we are not dealing with a different culture or a traumatic child-hood, despite the fact that these can certainly be important factors. Something in the psyche is missing or crippled. Something? Eros?

The man whose wife complained, "My husband is a psychopath," was well-adjusted socially. The other man, the fourth case who was found guilty of murder, was a criminal, an open enemy of society. They have something in common, although not their social adjustment or maladjustment. Both are psychopaths. Unfortunately psychopathy is often used synonymously with social maladjustment or criminality. Psychopathy, however, is not characterized by the degree of social adaptation nor by criminality. If both men have psychopathy in common, perhaps an exploration of what else they have in common will lead us to a better understanding of this particular form of inva-lidism.

Both are charming and intelligent, and both relate easily to other people on a superficial level. Both men seem to exhibit feelings or at least to act as if they had feelings. The man who committed murder could be friendly; once he even saved a swan from drowning in an oil slick. He often showed aggressive feelings as, for example, when he described how he had beaten someone to death. Mr. Socially Adjusted was also capable of showing feelings, particularly toward people with whom he was doing business. Such expressions, a kind of hail-fellow-well-met, came only as long as business was good. Those with whom he came in contact found him warm and friendly. Others who knew him well often felt him to be insincere and hollow.

Both men had difficulty committing themselves and consequently were unable to establish long-term relationships. They could carry on a lively conversation with someone one minute and have forgotten that same person as soon as his back was turned. Their motto seemed to be, "Out of sight, out of mind." Relationships for them were things of the moment, passing things which could be taken up as the situation demanded. They never seemed to have the need to spend time with others on a frequent basis. They seldom wrote to acquaintances—if they were gone, they were gone. In the event that an acquaintance showed up after a long period of time, they could be just as charming and pleasant as at their last encounter. Relationships did not seem to be something that could be developed and enjoyed but were simply temporal necessities.

A *sense of morals* seemed also to be lacking in both men. They never had guilty consciences, they were never ashamed of what they had done, and never regretted acts they had committed, even when such acts hurt others. Both were liars. Speech was not a means of expressing truth, but a tool to achieve whatever was needed. What they said reflected the exigencies of the situation rather than their own thoughts or feelings. They had no concept of truth, and so no one could ever trust them, whether the promises they made were important ones or not. "I'll visit you tomorrow in the hospital," was no more an indication that such a visit would take place than the words, "I'll pay you back your $30,000 in two weeks," meant that such payment would ever occur.

Both men were egoistic, thinking only of themselves, how they could best use a situation to their advantage, and what was in it for them. It was impossible for them to love someone or to care for someone other than themselves.

Both the socially adjusted and the socially maladjusted man knew what they were doing; they did not lack insights into their behavior. At the same time any such insight was as transient as were their relationships. The successful businessman made the following assessment of his family life: "I really feel sorry for my wife. I guess I should be more considerate of my family. From now on I'll try and spend more time with them. We could go swimming or hiking every Saturday. I understand how important it is." However when the following Saturday arrived, nothing happened. All his understanding was useless since it was never translated into action.

Both men led relatively *normal sex lives*. Both had their first sexual experience between the ages of thirteen and fourteen. This is somewhat early. Sexual relations are only allowed by law in Switzerland after the age of sixteen, and most men seldom have their first experience before this age. This is not due to legal restrictions, but because inhibitions and scruples involved with sexuality are only sufficiently dealt with between the ages of sixteen and twenty. These two men had no such scruples. For them sexuality was a way of satisfying a need, much as one drinks a glass of water to satisfy one's thirst. Both did exhibit latent tendencies to polymorphous perversity, another way of saying that it did not matter how their sexual needs were met, whether heterosexual or homosexual, and the businessman tended toward sadism. They certainly never worried about sexuality. While they were both potent, sexuality did not seem to mean that much to them: it was neither positive nor negative. One could almost say that their sexuality was ideal, without any pronounced complications.

Their *relationship to reality* was good. Neither suffered from delusions or illusions of any kind. The murderer was extremely distrustful, and now and again he would justify his own aggressive behavior by attributing to others motives or intentions which did not exist. As a rule he was able to perceive reality as it was.

Neither man was neurotic. Neither demonstrated particular anxieties, compulsions, or neurotic moodiness. Only the most exhaustive psychological examination could have revealed even the traces of a neurosis. To a certain extent both men were extremely healthy. They ate and slept well and awoke each morning feeling refreshed and ready to go. Nor was either man mentally ill. Neither showed any pronounced or clear psychiatric symptoms. Their inability to form lasting relationships, to commit themselves to another person, was so blatant that one could easily conceive that this difficulty might eventually result in some form of mental disorder.

A close look at the two men's life histories revealed something quite curious: there seemed to be no *psychological development*. They were the same at age six as they were at ten, twenty, or thirty. At least that is what those who knew them well maintained. The one was always polite and unreliable, the other brutal and aggressive. A classmate who had known the businessman at the age of fifteen and met him fifteen years later said, "He is still the same. He hasn't changed in the least." One even got the impression that their faces had stayed the same over the years, remaining smooth and unwrinkled as if the passing of time had made no impression upon them, had left no indication of any kind of psychic development. To some extent we all remain the same: our sixth-grade classmate whom we meet thirty years later looks astonishingly like we remember him. Yet this is only one side of our experience of others since we also see how much another has changed. Every experience leaves its mark—seniors in high school often look much different after their graduation, and many men and women change quickly after their wedding.

Both men could act as if they *cared for others*. You might say they were highly talented actors to whom noble gestures came easily. One time when the businessman was still at university, he brought his hostess a huge bouquet of flowers. As it turned out he had stolen the flowers from the neighbor's garden. Another time he brought along a large box of chocolates purchased with money he had borrowed from a friend and which he never repaid. Such were his "noble gestures." The murderer was an animal lover who became furious whenever he saw animals suffering or being tortured. There was even an article written about him in the local paper because of his dedication.

Both men were able to imitate (I said they were talented actors) *actions which expressed morality,* even to the point where others believed them. Here we have the same question that crops up with actors. Someone who plays a certain role has to understand it. But how far does this understanding go? Does it influence one's way of living? I do not know about actors, but I do know that these two men could play the role of "honorable men" without the word "honor" meaning anything at all to them. It often seemed that they were capable of sacrificing their own interests. The one who brought his hostess the flowers had occasional attacks of generosity. While a student he met a refugee in Zürich to whom he gave the last one hundred francs he had, although he was in severe financial straits. This was an impressive gesture. The next day he borrowed two hundred francs from another student which he never repaid.

As a businessman he could deliver the most touching and moving speeches. At a friend's wedding reception, he gave the bride a leather-bound book of poetry. He explained that he had seen the book and admired the poems the first time he had ever visited his friend. He took the book home with him, intending to return it later. In time he became so fond of it, that he simply could not part with it. Also it had become a symbol for him of his relationship with this friend. But now, he continued, his friend had married, and it was only appropriate that he return the book to the friend's new bride as a token of his friendship. Tears welled up in his eyes as he addressed the bride and groom. All the guests were deeply moved. The true story, however, was somewhat different. He had stolen the book from his friend's parents' library, because he had to write a book report for school. By chance he discovered it the day before the wedding and thought to bring it along to save himself the expense of a wedding present.

I have described two cases: a successful businessman and a brutal murderer. On the surface the two men appear completely different. I have emphasized their similarities, but have left out something else they have in common: both men are *liabilities* for society. This is apparent with the murderer but equally as serious in the case of the businessman. His family, partners, business associates, and acquaintances were disappointed, wronged, and hurt, not by any criminal acts, but by his selfishness, lack of concern, and inability to love. In fact those who showed concern for him were the ones he hurt the most.

We all know men and women with characteristics similar to these two men. Here a word of warning. I do not wish to moralize. I am not a Pharisee. It is not my intention to speak of "us" as different from "them," the psychopaths. I am concerned with the significance of psychopathy for human psychology in general. The men I have described are of importance for all of us as a psychological phenomenon, because everyone suffers from this form of psychic invalidism called psychopathy.

CHAPTER FIVE
Psychopaths in Literature

Psychopathic behavior frequently becomes the subject of literary endeavor, a subject which particularly fascinates novelists. One eighteenth-century author who was attracted by this phenomenon was Daniel Defoe, the author of *Robinson Crusoe*. He also wrote *Moll Flanders*, the story of a woman who had one adventure after another, now as a thief, now as a prostitute, and now as something else. By lying and cheating she always managed to come out on top. She always seemed to improve her situation, but the more she "improved," the worse she became morally. One time, for example, she admitted to one of her patrons that she was a terrible woman and that she deeply regretted her misdeeds. Tears streamed down her cheeks; the man was moved, a careless indulgence on his part since she used the opportunity to relieve him of his billfold.

Curiously Defoe seems to side with his heroine, describing her in such a way that the reader cannot help but sympathize with her. Reading the scene where she steals her benefactor's wallet, one thinks, "Serves him right, the sentimental old fool! He deserves to be robbed!" Our sympathies are aroused despite the moral conflict. I will say more about this later.

Oscar Wilde offers a profound description of a psychopath in his novel *The Picture of Dorian Gray*. In the novel a portrait is painted of the protagonist and is placed in the attic. The protagonist behaves abysmally, seducing young women, betraying friends, and so forth and so on. He never ages, however. His face remains the same, that of a handsome young man. Only the portrait in the attic is affected, becoming uglier and uglier until one day Dorian Gray stabs the portrait with a knife, and he himself dies. The portrait undergoes a transformation while the protagonist does what he wants, untouched and unpunished by his deeds. He does not know fear and sadness. Parenthetically, fear and sadness are two emotions which are foreign to psychopaths, one reason why they are often heroic soldiers.

The social-climbing psychopath is the subject of Guy de Maupassant's novel, *Belami*. Belami, the protagonist, is incapable of love but builds a career for himself with the aid of women whom he pretends to love. Cynical and immoral, he plays the outraged moralist in articles he writes as a journalist. The only thing that matters for him is success and social recognition. Nothing is as important to such amoral and asocial individuals as social recognition, a paradox about which more will be said.

I was once asked whether the figure of Raskolnikoff in Dostoyevski's *Crime and Punishment* could be seen as a psychopath. While the answer is "no," I am tempted to say that Raskolnikoff was a young man who tried to be a psychopath, doubting the strength of his moral convictions and trying to overcome them without success. He was very moral. He killed an old woman—a helpless, complaining, unpleasant old hag—who was of no use to herself or anyone else. Raskolnikoff tried to convince himself that the old woman's death did not hurt anyone since she was such a useless creature. He began to feel guilty, was sentenced, and accepted his punishment as just. He is not at all a psychopath, even though he committed murder; killing the old woman was not the act of a psychopath. He was fascinated by the deed, by the horror of murder, using it to explore what morality and humanity actually are. Here lies the difference. It is not the deed which makes a person a psychopath, but ones relationship to it. The brutal murder of the old woman could well be interpreted as psychopathic. However it depends in what frame of mind the deed was committed. Even the most apparently immoral action can reflect highly moral convictions as was the case with Raskolnikoff.

Raskolnikoff's may be an extreme example, but we notice similar attempts among adolescents to probe the nature of our moral being, to discover what ethics really are. Most of them, to be sure, break off the experiment before it reaches the extreme of murder. Still many youths commit acts which seem to be psychopathic, but which more accurately should be classified with Raskolnikoff's searching and questioning. They are deeds intended to explore the boundaries and reaches of human morality.

From its beginnings literature has reported on this curious form of invalidism which we call psychopathy.

ADOLF GUGGENBÜHL-CRAIG

Certainly our fascination for the phenomenon lies in the fact that when we study psychopathy, we learn about our own psychopathic natures, realize our invalidism, and our limits. It forces us to consider why we are not amoral in spite of the fact that we have tendencies to amorality within us. We consider our feelings, asking ourselves about the nature of ethics and love. Psychopathy is a tool with which we can better understand ourselves.

CHAPTER SIX
The Development of the Term Psychopathy

Certainly psychopathy as a phenomenon is as old as humanity, and anyone who regards human beings as basically good and moral must deal with the unloving, immoral aspects which find expression in each of us. Perhaps one of the earliest descriptions of psychopathy is found in the *Bible* in the book of *Deuteronomy* 21:18-21:

> If a man has a stubborn and rebellious son, who will not obey the voice of his father or the voice of his mother, and, though they chastise him, will not give heed to them, then his father and his mother shall take hold of him and bring him out to the elders of his city at the gate of the place where he lives, and they shall say to the elders of his city, "Our son is stubborn and rebellious, he will not obey our voice; he is a glutton and drunkard." Then all the men of the city shall stone him to death with stones; so you shall purge the evil from your midst; and all Israel shall hear, and fear. (Revised Standard Edition)

The son described in this passage must be a case with no hope of change or improvement; otherwise his parents would not be called upon to deliver him to his death. It is this hopelessness which leads us to suspect that the passage concerns psychopathy. The note of hopelessness evokes the image of "eternal damnation," a concept which is probably related to the psychopathic side of humans in twofold fashion. First there are certain people or certain sides of people which cannot be saved or cured; second humanity's religion or mythology has always designated certain individuals who, of necessity, are abandoned to damnation. The Calvinist doctrine of predestination is a case in point. The classical concept of Hell may well have been intended for psychopaths but also expresses the psychopathic side of believers who have to resolve the fact that while they sing with the heavenly choirs, the sinners suffer the fire and brimstone of Hell's damnation. It has only been since the French Revolution that doctors, and not primarily theologians, have turned their attention to psychopathy. It is assumed that the famous psychiatrist Philippe Pinel (1745-1826), who released the mentally ill from dungeons in which they had been confined, was the first to describe psychopathy as a psychiatric phenomenon. Pinel spoke of an *emportement maniaque sans délire,* a diagnosis intended to describe those exhibiting none of the classical symptoms of mental illness, but whose behavior was marked by cruelty, criminality, sexual perversion, alcoholism, addiction, irresponsibility, and immorality. Pinel found that the intelligence of such individuals was generally high, that they were "rational," could think well, but something was not quite right. He originally felt that mental illness did not exist without delusions, illusions, and altered consciousness. However he then discovered cases with none of the usual disturbances of thinking and perception, but where feeling and morality were disturbed.

Jean Etienne Dominique Esquirol (1772-1840), one of Pinel's students, introduced the concept of *folie raisonante* or *folie morale*, defined as *des altérations de la volonté et des sentiments, l'intélligence conservante son integrité* (alteration of intention and feeling where the intelligence retains its integrity). The syndrome was observed primarily among criminals. In 1835 the English psychiatrist James C. Prichard (1786-1848) wrote about "moral insanity" and "moral imbecility." Prichard assumed that there were individuals who suffered from an inherited lack of a sense of morality.

When we hear the term psychopathy today, in the back of our minds we hear "moral insanity," even though we might not be versed in the history of psychiatry. The history and development of many psychiatric terms still plays an important role in our contemporary understanding. Behind "schizophrenia" lurks "dementia praecox," which, before Bleuler renamed the condition, implied a disorder which began among young people and ended in total senility. This accounts for many of the negative connotations which schizophrenia has for us today.

When James Prichard spoke of "moral insanity," he meant a mental disorder in which the so-called "natural" feelings, affects, and moods were perverse. He observed a confusion of the moral side of the entire personality without this confusion affecting the intelligence. He was impressed by the presence of an average or even above-average level of intelligence in these individuals. He was convinced that there were as many varieties of "moral insanity" as there were feelings and emotions. He believed that each feeling could be undermined by a corresponding perversion, and therefore one should speak of "moral insanity." Although these varieties of feelings or moral perversions are due to improper or inappropriate thinking, according to Prichard the afflicted individuals, no matter how shocking and repulsive, are intellectually healthy.

Apparently Prichard described a phenomenon similar to the one I have portrayed in cases three and four. Yet the six cases that Prichard cited to prove his theory were, as we now know, *not* morally insane. One of the cases he described was that of an unspecific psychosis; another became schizophrenic. The third case turned out to be manic-depressive, while the fourth suffered from syphilis. The remaining two cases later developed symptoms of severe compulsion neuroses. That not one of Prichard's "moral insanity" cases was actually what he said it was does not detract from his outstanding research.

We assume that, as a rule, scientists or doctors come to certain conclusions and establish particular theories on the basis of their observations. I have the impression that it works the other way around. Someone has an idea—in psychiatry most likely on the basis of self-observation—and then tries to find support for the idea in what is observed. One might be unlucky and place the idea or theory where it does not actually belong, just as Prichard labeled individuals "morally insane" even though according to his own definition, that was not their affliction. Therefore it is not so important that Prichard incorrectly diagnosed his cases. His concept might still be applicable and of psychological significance.

In the United States Benjamin Rush (1745-1813) has been called the "first American psychiatrist" to recognize the phenomenon of psychopathy. He was a great reformer of American mental institutions, but even great reformers have their dark sides. He invented a revolving chair where patients were placed and spun around until they became terribly dizzy, a rather brutal form of therapy. Supposedly some patients were cured by this method. Rush assumed that the Will could be diseased and that there were individuals who, despite normal intelligence and capabilities, could be suffering from an illness of Will. He described cases in which the sense of morality was disturbed, but where the intelligence was quite high. He was fascinated by people who, like the murderer and the businessman described above, were intelligent, could carry on pleasant conversations, readily grasp the moral aspects of any discussion, and at the same time could act in the most immoral fashion much to the detriment of other people.

Why were men like Pinel, Esquirol, Prichard, and Rush so drawn to the condition they described as "*emportement maniaque sans deliré*" or "moral insanity?" These men all lived at the close of the Age of Enlightenment, a period in which intelligence, rationality, and the ability to think were viewed as the determining characteristics of humanity. Intelligence was considered the highest and most human quality. If intelligence, if the intellect were in order, so these enlightened ones thought, then the rest of the human being had to be in order, functioning properly. According to their philosophy it was not possible that someone could think properly and act immorally—it contradicted their image of humanity. It was assumed that moral qualities and the ability to live and work in harmony with society resulted from a well-functioning intellect. Morality was understood to be connected to or the result of intelligence. Prior to the Enlightenment, morality was viewed as a kind of revelation. Consequently, to find individuals with good intelligence and bad morality fascinated and puzzled these sons of the Enlightenment.

Though that was one hundred and fifty years ago, still the linking of morality and intelligence haunts the thinking of doctor and layman alike. Now and then a newspaper reporter writes that it is ". . . particularly astounding to see how such an intelligent man could behave in such a criminal fashion." Or one hears the expression, "How can he behave so badly and be so smart?" That intelligent individuals could perform immoral or asocial actions was a shocking paradox for the Age of Enlightenment and forced a rethinking of the entire problem of evil and destruction decidedly influenced by the concept of moral insanity. The results are still apparent in our penal code to this day.

A basic concept of penal law is that mentally disturbed individuals are not responsible for their deeds. The idea goes back to Roman Law which, having spread throughout Europe, gradually lost relevancy in practical significance toward the end of the Middle Ages. However introduce into the situation the concept of "moral insanity," and the potential complications become almost endless. A lawbreaker is punished for numerous reasons: one of these is deterrence. Another reason for punishment, one we often forget, is revenge. Should a major crime go unpunished, unrevenged, the average, law-abiding citizen would feel frustrated and angry. Crimes, like sins, cannot go unrevenged without threatening the order of human existence. Atonement is also an important element of punishment. Something morally wrong is committed, and the offender should repent and atone for the act in order to be rehabilitated. Deterrence, repentance, and atonement (although not revenge) presuppose free will. It is presumed that individuals who commit crimes are capable of realizing that they have done something wrong and then are able to act on this understanding. If individuals do not recognize wrongdoing, then deterrence, atonement, and repentance—and the basis for punishment—are totally pointless.

Then what happens when the concept of moral insanity is applied in the sentencing of criminal acts? The foundations of the entire penal code begin to tremble. If the moral side of individuals can be "mentally ill," then they are no longer responsible for their deeds and can no longer be punished. Even though such criminals might be able to think normally, act rationally, and recognize what is and what is not reality, they cannot be punished since their sense of morality is diseased, disturbed, and deficient. Since it appears that a large number of criminals suffer from moral deficiency, in the final analysis only a limited number could be justifiably punished. The end result would be that only morally gifted individuals could or should be punished.

The concept of moral insanity has been the cause of unrest among scholars. Many have shaken a warning finger and pointed out that the notion undermines our entire social structure and threatens law and moral order. Each misdeed, so they argue, could in the future be interpreted as the expression of mental disease and thus bring punishment of any sort to an end. They maintain that "moral insanity" could serve to excuse the most heinous crimes and to protect the malefactors from making retribution. Consequently some psychiatrists have limited the term "moral insanity" to apply only to cases in which brain damage is present. Should a criminal act and the so-called moral insanity not result from brain damage, from a tumor or high fever, for example, then the deed could not be excused on the basis of mental illness and should accordingly be punished.

Clerics and the theological establishment fought the concept of moral insanity. Consider, they suggested, that humanity's greatest challenge has been to live a moral life, to obey the Ten Commandments. If someone said that those who obeyed the Ten Commandments were healthy and everyone else sick, the entire moral-religious system would collapse like a house of cards. You would no longer need to be responsible for your existence; you could simply plead that one was sick.

I have mentioned criminal law to show that the notion of moral insanity, the predecessor of psychopathy, challenges many of our psychological as well as personal assumptions. It jeopardizes our moral system, our legal code, and the image of ourselves as moral beings.

At the beginning of the nineteenth century, the soul was conceived as an homogeneous entity. As soon as it was observed, however, that the intellect could be healthy while the same individual was mentally disturbed in the sense of moral deficiency, the homogeneity of the soul was at an end. Today we might find the shock and surprise of those living at that time somewhat curious. Most modern psychologists assume that the soul consists of many different parts. For doctors in those days, however, the concept of a fragmented soul was earth-shaking. One should remember that during the Middle Ages people saw how fragmented the soul really is. There was talk of demons which possessed or angels which protected. At least phenomenologically, the heterogeneity of the soul was described in detail. Admittedly it is not the same thing to see that an individual is possessed by demons as to accept that the same demon is part of the soul of the one possessed. The belief in demons and angels was still a recognition that the human soul had to be understood as a manifold, heterogeneous entity. Then came the Enlightenment, and angels and demons were renounced in favor of the oneness of the soul, a belief shared by many even today. For the Enlightenment, then, the oneness of the soul was an achievement, a milestone on the road of human progress and development.

Investigators who were convinced that there was such a thing as "moral insanity" held that it was meaningful to speak of an aptitude for morality. A sense of morality was understood to be a talent, a quantum which was either large, medium, or small, but which could also be disturbed or absent altogether. Opponents of moral insanity maintained that a sense of morality could not be separated from intelligence. They attempted to prove that in every case of moral insanity the intelligence of the individual in question was impaired. They were never successful in the endeavor but would not give up trying.

Defenders of the moral insanity theory even attempted to employ phrenology to support their arguments. Phrenology is a pseudo-science in which characteristics of the soul may be determined on the basis of facial and skull features. If the back of the skull is large, for example, it indicates a high degree of morality in an individual. If the back of the skull is not large, the phrenologists believed the person had only minimal moral ability. Phrenology is still practiced today to some extent. People with high foreheads are believed to be intelligent, while those with low foreheads are supposed to be ignorant. Even the notion that flatness of the back of the head indicates a lack of morality prevails among some contemporaries. Using phrenology to support the concept of moral insanity is circular thinking. If you can tell from the shape of the skull whether or not an individual has moral aptitude, you can conclude that there is such a thing as moral aptitude.

Supporters of moral insanity went a step further: moral aptitude, they claimed, is something one is born with. You are either morally gifted or totally bereft of moral aptitude at birth. "Words, words, words," responded the opponents. "Intelligence and morality are but words and correspond in no way with physical or psychic reality. We describe different aspects of the soul with words since those are the only tools at our command. Actually, however, the soul is homogeneous, even if we use words to label different 'parts' of it."

During the nineteenth century the physical indicators of moral insanity became more and more important. In 1878 a French doctor, Monz Gouster, suggested that "moral insanity cases" were characterized by asymmetrical skull formation and large ears. There are still those who believe that overly large ears indicate negative character traits. The discussion came to a head at the close of the century during a conference of the Italian Phreniatric Society in Rome. The theme of the congress was "Moral Insanity." Much of what we know now about psychopathy and everything that the nineteenth century had to say about the topic was discussed at this congress. Most of the participants understood "moral insanity" as a designation for an individual who could intellectually grasp the idea of moral and social obligations, but who could not relate to or live by these values. They all agreed that the phenomenon existed, but explaining it was a different matter entirely.

Some regarded the morally insane individual as almost identical to the born criminal as described by the Italian criminologist Cesare Lombroso (1836-1909). Moral insanity should be understood as an atavism. Rather than being a disease, it occurred in cases where the brain was insufficiently developed, whether due to a disease or some other reason. As a result of the retarded brain development, the individual was unable effectively to integrate a moral sense and could not appreciate its importance. In a somewhat contrived fashion, Lombroso differentiated between the born criminal and the morally insane individual. The latter simply lacked the psychic components which determine morality. He felt that the born criminal should be termed a degenerate with moral abilities which had deteriorated and degenerated. Further, Lombroso claimed, the born criminal is characterized by a prominent jaw, large ears, and a low forehead. This is not true of the morally insane. The born criminal is generally left-handed and exhibits a high degree of motor coordination. The latter observation is interesting since today we frequently attribute coordination to psychopaths, the "descendants" of the morally insane.

Carlo Bonuomo, another Italian doctor, supported a different perspective. He believed our moral and social sense is simply a product of our society. He was of the opinion that the sense of morality depends on the culture in which one is raised. This explained why different social classes espoused differing moral values. Bonuomo's idea, that our moral values merely result from our environment's effect, is a popular position today and finds many defenders. Bonuomo was even more specific, claiming that moral insanity was due to improper upbringing. That should sound familiar to us—"It is all the parents' fault."

All of these psychiatrists and doctors were conscientious in their observations and believed firmly that they arrived at their theories on the basis of their observations. Looking at their reports today, we can see at once how strongly fantasy entered into their theories. It is apparent that these investigators did not derive their ideas simply from observation but measured criminality on the basis of jaw bones; those without prominent jaws could not, therefore, be criminal. In retrospect we can see how much the nineteenth-century scientists mixed reality and fantasy. Another example comes from the United States where researchers maintained that only white, Anglo-Saxon Protestants could suffer from moral insanity. We now know that this is not so. However, white, Anglo-Saxon Protestants were the only subjects examined by these researchers, therefore . . .

In England Joseph Wiglesworth asserted that moral insanity could only be found in civilized cultures and not among so-called primitive ones, since *all* primitives were morally insane. Another way of looking at this statement is that the morally insane are our "primitives." Wiglesworth assumed that all human beings were originally lacking in morality, a quality which was only achieved in the course of cultural and social development. The researchers who accepted this and similar theories had only limited knowledge of the psychology of so-called primitives. Today we realize how absurd it is to regard primitive cultures as morally insane or psychopathic.

I would like to reemphasize that I do not regard the admixture of fantasy and observation, the introduction of subjective fantasy into observed actualities, as illegitimate. There has been much written on the need for subjectivity in psychological and psychiatric work. The nineteenth century and the first part of the twentieth were extremely fruitful in the field of psychology and psychiatry for the very reason that researchers were not so concerned about exactness in their methodology, or about confusing fantasy, projection, and so-called hard facts in their work. However, beginning with the turn of the century, fantasy and wild theories began more and more to be replaced by a more scientific, empirical approach. The shocking term "moral insanity" evolved under German influence into the more neutral "psychopathic inferiority" and finally to psychopathy.

The development of the diagnosis "psychopathy" differed in the English-speaking countries from Germany. While the Germans associated the condition more with criminality, the English and Americans had a broader-based understanding of the syndrome. Adolf Meier (1866-1950), a Swiss psychiatrist working in America, used the term "constitutional inferiority." In 1914 Karl Bierbaum wrote about "psychopathic criminals." The intelligence of such individuals could be quite high and could somewhat offset the lack of a moral sense and even enable a degree of social adaptation.

Emil Kraepelin (1856-1926), often called the Chancellor of Imperial German Psychiatry and an admirer of Bismarck, nick-named the Iron Chancellor, described psychopaths as being "inferior in their feeling life and in the development of their Will." He claimed that life was difficult for them because of insufficiencies in the areas of emotion and volition. Psychopaths demonstrated a lack of temperance in all areas of their personality.

My view of psychiatry in general and psychopathy in particular has been conditioned by the Bleulers, Eugen, and Manfred. In the 1955 edition of his psychiatric textbook, Manfred, then chief of staff of the Cantonal Psychiatric Hospital in Zürich, the Burghoelzli, gave the description of psychopathy which is most generally accepted. It is a clear and concise definition. He writes that psychopathy is a "congenital character variant, which leads to social difficulties and personal suffering." We see from this how much broader the term has become. It is no longer identical with moral debility, that being only one possibility of the syndrome. Manfred Bleuler regarded psychopaths as people who, from birth, are strange or odd, characteristics which cause both the individuals and those around them difficulties. Yet it is not the nature of one's character which makes up a psychopath, but that the character causes personal suffering as well as social problems. Bleuler emphasizes that though it can appear that psychopaths are but a product of their environment, such is not the case. As a rule, he continues, psychopaths have a negative influence from the beginning on their environment, even though the reverse may seem to hold true. As children, psychopaths can relate to their mothers only to a limited extent and may, for this reason, be rejected by her. They do not become psychopaths because their mothers reject them but the other way around. They are rejected because they are psychopaths, and something in their character repels their environment.

Bleuler further points out that brain damage due to illness or accident may result in syndromes similar to psychopathy. The reverse does not, of course, hold true: those suffering from brain damage do not always exhibit the characteristics of psychopathy. I am not pointing this out simply for its theoretical interest. Minimal brain damage may frequently be diagnosed in children with behavioral problems but is no indication that they are psychopaths.

As I have already mentioned, Bleuler emphasizes the congenital nature of the psychopathic character, a phenomenon of interest not only in connection with psychopathy but for psychology in general. Are we born like the *tabula rasa* which John Locke, the seventeenth-century English philosopher, described like a lump of warm sealing wax where the passage of time and experience leaves its imprint? Or are characteristics, traits, and peculiarities of each individual already present at the time of birth? Which factor is a greater determinant in human development: inheritance or the influence of the environment? The question is summed up in the English expression, "Nature against Nurture." To pose the question in this "either/or" manner seems unpsychological to me. If it were possible to explain our individual uniqueness by heredity and environmental influence, there would not seem to be any room left for the independence of the soul. There must be another factor, a third element, which is neither inherited nor explainable on the basis of outside influence.

In his psychiatric text Bleuler presents a list of the different types of psychopaths. I would remind the reader that the English psychiatrist Prichard assumed that there were as many different forms of "moral insanity" as there were character traits. German psychiatrists also set up long lists of the various kinds of psychopaths. I would like briefly to describe the types that Bleuler recorded in order to provide an idea of what is called psychopathic behavior.

There are the so-called unstable psychopaths, those who are subject to the slightest influence, who change their minds from one minute to the next, and who cannot be counted on. They are like dry leaves in the wind, blowning this way and that. Bleuler also describes the *attention-seeking types* who are always trying to appear better than they are. Often confidence artists or imposters, they never suffer from pangs of conscience. There are also the so-called *sensitive psychopaths*, similar to some extent to Kretschmer's "sensitive" character form. These are people who are easily offended and touchy, who are always insulted, distrustful, suspecting enemies in everyone they meet. Any passing comment is interpreted as if it were intended for them as an expression of ill will. As a rule they are outsiders and bear up poorly under life's cruelties. They are narcissistic and egoistic, and while they are easily insulted, they never notice when they have insulted others.

Another type of psychopath is what Bleuler terms the *unemotional,* in which we recognize qualities of "moral insanity." They seldom show any feeling. It is uncomfortable to spend time with these people, or one feels a kind of internal emptiness since the people themselves bring nothing to the relationship. Bleuler labels a further type *eccentric.* While they are not actually sick or schizophrenic, their thinking processes are odd, and one has difficulty identifying with them on an emotional level. They seem to live in a kind of delusional state, to have a good sense of reality but never to be quite in harmony with their environment and those around them. Many are members of religious sects or extremist political parties. They are often laughed at, rejected, or even despised for their eccentricity.

In Bleuler's list we find the entry, *pseudologia fantastica,* people who continually lie without having any real reason for doing so. Their relationship to truth is so disturbed that lying becomes a compulsive necessity even where they would be better served by telling the truth. They lie whether it is to their advantage or not. *Fantastica* does not imply that what they say is so out of the ordinary. Ask them, for example, "Where did you go today?" and the answer is, "Oh, I went shopping. The first two stores were closed, and I had to go to a third one to get what I needed." In reality, one later discovers, none of the stores were closed. Or, one of these people might say he had been to Berlin, and we ask how the weather was. "It rained the entire time," could be the answer, when it was really clear and sunny. The lie seems totally pointless and compulsive.

Pseudologia fantastica sounds rather exotic and is a condition which is relatively rare. On the other hand we frequently encounter *pseudologia*, lying without the compulsive component. Many of us do not pay too much attention to what is true and what is untrue, not because we are necessarily immoral, but because truth is not something which is highly valued. "He is a stranger to the truth," as the English say. It is often quite a while before another's untruthfulness is recognized. In some form or other truth, even if we lie now and then, is considered important, but just as some people are color-blind, some are also blind to the truth.

The somewhat outmoded diagnosis, *Neurasthenia*, is also considered a form of psychopathy. Neurasthenics tire quickly and are just as quick to anger. They are described as nervous and somewhat devoid of feeling. Yet another form of psychopathy is the *spendthrift*, one who cannot seem to hold on to anything. Material possessions mean nothing to them; they live from one day to the next. No sooner do they have something than they squander it and are consequently always in need. Bleuler also describes the *wanderer type*, vagrants who can no more stay in one place than with one relationship. Hoboes frequently fall into this category. Then there are the *chronically quarrelsome*, people who are at odds with everyone everywhere. These individuals are frequently

71

encountered in courts of law, bouncing from one law-suit to the next, quarreling their way through life.

Bleuler also classifies psychopaths from the per-spective of the psychoses. For example there is the *schizoid psychopath,* a term which does not imply schizophrenia or mental disease, but rather charac-teristics which are in some way analogous to schizophrenia. This type of person is cool, withdrawn, and split-off from his feeling life. Bleuler talks about *cyclical psychopaths,* those demonstrating traits of cy-clical psychosis, of the *manic-depressive* syndrome with the lows of depression and the highs of mania. While they are subject to emotional swings, the varia-tion is not as severe as in cases of manic-depressive psychosis and does not interfere significantly with their contact with reality.

Another expression, *epileptoid psychopath*, is used although rather infrequently. Epilepsy fascinated psy-chiatrists of the nineteenth century who for a long time postulated such a thing as the "epileptic personal-ity." They assumed that in addition to the characteristic seizures, epileptics exhibited particular traits like de-pendency and an overdeveloped sense of justice, as well as a tendency toward unrestrained emotional outbursts. An epileptoid psychopath, then, would be a person with characteristics similar to the epileptic personality.

Bleuler also mentions the *chronic ethical deviations* among the varieties of psychopathy (constitutional ethical deviations, asocial or antisocial personalities, moral feeblemindedness, moral idiots, and imbeciles,* and "moral insanity"). Although he applied the category primarily to criminals, he emphasized that the diagnosis was a catchall and that numerous factors contribute to criminality. Phenomenologically the widest variation is found in types of criminals: chance criminals, habitual criminals, professional criminals, and premeditated criminals.

Sexual perversions are only listed as an associated phenomenon in the 1955 edition of Bleuler's text. I would again remind the reader that psychopathy is a congenital or inborn character variant which leads to social difficulties and personal suffering. Until thirty or forty years ago, many psychiatrists felt that sexual perversion should be categorized as a form of psychopathy. Perversions like homosexuality, pedophilia, transvestism, exhibitionism, fetishism, nymphomania, satyriasis, priapism, sodomy, sadomasochism, etc. were considered to be congenital. It was believed that these variants never changed, but because they mellowed with age, they became less pronounced and less of a problem for the individual and his environment. The influence of Freud's theories of sexuality changed these views to the point where sexual perversions are regarded only to a limited extent as being psychopathic. Today developmental factors are seen as being more important.

---

*Translator's note: These are psychiatric designations of degrees of mental retardation which pre-date the World Health Organization's re-classification and may not be familiar to the reader as such.

ADOLF GUGGENBÜHL-CRAIG

As you can see from what has already been said, the diagnosis "psychopathy" has been exaggerated out of proportion. The slightest quirk or kink in the human personality which could not be reduced to some specific cause like brain damage or a traumatic childhood was labeled psychopathy. The World Health Organization has found a compromise definition for psychopathy as stated in the *International Classification of Diseases* (*ICD*). Under #301 (diagnoses are specified by number) we find the "Personality Disorders" described as follows:

> Deeply ingrained maladaptive patterns of behavior generally recognizable by the time of adolescence or earlier and continuing throughout most of adult life, although often becoming less obvious in middle or old age. The personality is abnormal either in the balance of its components, their quality and expression or in its total aspect. Because of this deviation or psychopathy the patient suffers or others have to suffer and there is an adverse effect upon the individual or society. It includes what is sometimes called psychopathic personality, but if this is determined primarily by malfunctioning of the brain, it should not be classified here . . . (*ICD*, 1975 revision).

What was once considered "congenital" is now spoken of as "ingrained." Category #301 contains the following subdivisions: #301.0 "Paranoid Personality Disorder," #301.1 "Affective Personality Disorder," #301.2 "Schizoid

74

Personality Disorder," #301.3 "Explosive Personality Disorder," #301.4 "Anankastic Personality Disorder," #301.5 "Hysterical Personality Disorder," #301.6 "Asthenic Personality Disorder," #301.7 "Personality Disorders with Predominantly Sociopathic or Asocial Manifestations," #301.8 "Other Personality Disorders," and #301.9 "Unspecified." The diagnosis "Psychopathic Personality" forms a part of #301.9. Sexual deviations and disorders are separate from the personality disorders but follow them directly as #302.

All these different lists of psychopathies are fascinating, offering as they do a sort of rogues gallery of human nature. What is missing, however, is a system, some dynamic principle which would draw the various parts together. The lists are more a hodgepodge of curios, a gathering of sideshow attractions. They are reminiscent of the history books of the Middle Ages which relate one event after another for the sake of narration but without any particular connection. Yet it is just the unsystematic nature of these lists of characterological possibilities which is so advantageous when compared to distinct typologies. The trouble with typologies, including Jung's typology, is that they form closed systems allowing only for that which is given by the system. That is one danger, the other one being more insidious and destructive. Let us say we have diagnosed someone as an introverted feeling type. We then know exactly what this person is and stop observation. Anything which does not correspond to the diagnosis is simply rejected; the immediacy of observation and relationship is broken. On the other hand the lists of psychopathies make no claim to finality. The richness of the psychopathic character is not restricted just because it is left up to our fantasy to describe new forms of psychopathy.

Indeed it seems that the psychological importance of psychopathy is the extent to which it stimulates the imagination, a claim supported by the endless lists of psychopathies. For example psychodynamic principles have been applied to the understanding of psychopaths since 1925 with emphasis being on the psychogenetic aspects. Psychoanalytical schools believe that psychopaths are individuals fixated in an infantile stage of the first phallic phase. Sociologists, of course, view psychopaths as a sociological problem. Some have even seen fit to invent or discover their own name for the syndrome. Ben Cartmann (1935) restricted the designation to "primary" psychopathy, what he called *Anettopathy*. *Anettopaths* are extremely egoistic individuals with little feeling for others, narcissistic, without morals, mostly criminal, or generally asocial.

I am not interested in determining whether the psychodynamic interpretation—or any other interpretation—is correct or not. There are, and must be, numerous models for understanding the human psyche. What interests me is the perspective of those psychiatrists who applied the term psychopathy as Bleuler did. I am interested in the particular image of humanity which underlies the classical definition and description of Bleuler and his predecessors. Both the understanding of psychopathy and the reflection on human nature are widespread among physician and layman with, I would suggest, considerable justification.

CHAPTER SEVEN
Deserts of the Soul—Lacunae and Heredity

Psychiatric circles in the nineteenth and twentieth centuries viewed, and still view, human nature as an accumulation or an interaction of various abilities and capabilities developed to a greater or lesser degree or not at all. A particular characteristic or certain abilities may for all practical purposes be missing from birth. These absent or missing traits were/are labeled *lacunae*, unoccupied rooms in the house of the psyche. Imagine, if you will, a geography of the psyche, an immense continent peopled by different tribes (the abilities and capabilities) which live and develop accordingly. Following the analogy further, those areas which were uninhabited or uninhabitable, the deserts, barren areas, or *lacunae*, would represent psychopathies. Everyone has psychopathic traits; each of us is missing something or has some aspect that is markedly underdeveloped.

The image seems worth pursuing. For example many people are musically gifted while others are not quite so talented, and there are still others with no musical aptitude whatsoever. Musical aptitude could also be divided into various separate abilities like pitch, rhythm, and tone. However it would be going too far to regard a lack of musical ability as leading to social difficulties or even to personal suffering, unless one had the misfortune of being born into a highly musical family or society. If such were the case, the ungifted individual might suffer from having to sit through weekly concerts (personal suffering) and those around him from his inability to carry a tune (social suffering). Generally speaking, however, musicality is not a talent whose absence results in suffering.

Many professionals—doctors, social workers, teachers, and the like—reject the idea of psychic *lacunae*, of parts of the psyche which are missing. Music teachers will tell you that everyone can be musical—the potential is present in all of us and is either cultivated or buried. The same teacher who maintains that there is no such thing as an unmusical child battles daily with children in whom musicality is buried so deeply that it simply cannot be found. The emphasis is on cultivating and bringing out individual abilities but never on confronting and having it out with the notion that the ability in question may be lacking. While musicality is an important aspect of our lives, it is not determinative; something which cannot be said as far as moral ability or aptitude is concerned.

I find myself compelled in the course of this discussion to remind the reader constantly that I am not speaking of "us" and of "them," of us as integrated, balanced, or whole and of the others who are missing something—the psychopaths. Admittedly it is important to be able to recognize psychopathic individuals when we are confronted by them. It seems to me far more important that, in speaking of psychopathy, we strive to realize in what way we are psychopaths. The notion that there are *lacunae*—empty places— where each and every one of us is lacking in something is of significance. For example in every analysis, the point or the place is reached where the analysand in question has nothing, and we realize that it is pointless to wait until something develops or to demand that something should be there. In this particular area the analysand simply cannot understand or relate to the matter. Even if there is an understanding on the intellectual level, real understanding, a feeling connection, is not possible. What we do in analysis is to help analysands discover their individual *lacunae*, to know where they are. What makes the task so difficult is that individuals usually believe the empty places to be highly developed ones. They have so little understanding for these areas that they cannot see that there is nothing there. For example we all know how embarrassing it is to meet people who know absolutely nothing about acting, but who believe they do such wonderful impressions of people that they are painful in their ineptness. It is of utmost importance to apply the question of *lacunae* to ourselves: where are my *lacunae*? Where am I missing something?

But let us return to our subject. We have spoken of psychopathy as an inborn character variant which leads to personal and social suffering. Let us expand our inquiries by asking whether these variants are characterized solely by *lacunae* or whether an excess of certain character traits might not also lead to suffering and difficulties. Aggression—the ability to fight for something one believes in—varies from one individual to the next. When people are not aggressive enough, they suffer from their inability to assert themselves. When people are overly aggressive, they and those around them suffer, although for different reasons.

As mentioned above modern psychiatry has sought to avoid the diagnosis psychopathy. It has a bad press; it is almost profane. The term has been designated destructive, theoretically false, the source of misconceptions, and worst of all, unscientific. I find it difficult to understand such protests after having reviewed the background and history of psychopathy.

An important aspect of psychopathy is its finality, perhaps most pronounced in the theory of its congenital nature. The congenital quality, the role of inheritance, played an important part in the thinking of the nineteenth century and was even emphasized by Bleuler. Naturally there was always disagreement over the question of just what was inherited, how much and how little, but the concept of inheritance remained. We are born with or without a sense of morality, a moral aptitude, with or without the ability to love and be loved and so forth. It was this notion of the congenital and inherited nature of psychopathy which aroused such enmity and was labeled destructive. It is not difficult to see why. The notion contradicts the belief that all people are equal.

Liberté, Egalité, Fraternité. What happens to the ideal of equality if we are all born with different characters, if we all have differing personality traits or are lacking in certain traits even if such traits and their presence or absence were not related to a psychopathic personality? As long as we see ourselves as a *tabula rasa,* as starting life as a cleaned slate, equality has a chance. Imagine the theoretical complications if all people are created not equal but different. There could be no system, no social organization, no educational process which would restore or bring about equality. We would be different from birth! It is not hard to see why enlightenment influenced psychiatry had and has such difficulty with psychopathy.

We can also understand the anxiety that the concept of psychopathy could lead to serious misconceptions. How can we be certain whether someone is a psychopath or not? How can we know for sure whether difficulties with another person are caused by psychic *lacunae,* by deserts in that individual's soul or not? To accept the concept of psychopathy is to invite untold complications in our dealings with our fellow humans. How, for instance, do we deal with psychopathy when it is not merely a psychiatric diagnosis but another human being?

One disadvantage of psychopathy is that it gives us an excuse in our dealings with others. It gives us an excuse to stop trying. If despite all our therapeutic efforts we do not seem to be getting anywhere, we can always say, "Oh, well, this person must be a

81

psychopath. I can't do anything, because he just has too many *lacunae*." Perhaps this is the reason some people consider the idea of psychopathy to be immoral.

Psychiatry has the tendency to change common, harmless words into slurs and insults much as the vernacular does. Psychopathy has become such an insult in the same way as the term hysteria has. We all know the use of hysteria in contexts such as, "She's nothing but a hysterical woman!" When patients suffered from symptoms which were not explainable, they were promptly diagnosed "hysteric." At least it made the doctor feel better, even if it devalued patients and their problems. Doctors could wash their hands of the matter by placing the responsibility squarely and completely on the patient's shoulders. For some reason neutral diagnoses assume negative qualities and significance. This can be partially avoided by renaming or redefining the entire phenomenon or syndrome so that hysteria becomes "conversion reaction," or psychopathy becomes "Sociopathic Personality Disorder." The negative connotations of psychopathy can be alleviated through the use of the prefix "socio." At the same time the phenomenon under consideration becomes more harmless, since one is no longer dealing with the psyche, "psycho," but with a conflict between the individual and society.

It seems that psychopathy has affected completely unforeseeable areas. It has called attention to the theory of equality in philosophy and political science. The question of inheritance has further led to practical political considerations: some analysts have gone so far as to label the idea of inheritance in psychopathy fascist or at least *fascistoid*. Leftist-oriented psychotherapists maintain that inheritance has little or no importance for human beings: we are all born with the same potential. The dispute extends even to zoology where, it has been observed, animals are born with basic patterns of behavior. Consequently zoologists like Konrad Lorenz have been labeled fascist. Even Jung has been called a fascist, not because of the misplaced charges of anti-semitism, but because he maintained that human beings are born with certain patterns of behavior called archetypes.

People use the term fascism loosely these days. In point of fact it designated particular political movements of a dictatorial and elitist nature found primarily in Italy, Spain, and Romania. Fascism is often confused with National Socialism in Germany, a movement with fascist qualities but having distinctive and different elements such as the idea of master race.

Therefore, those of leftist persuasion tend to espouse the *tabula rasa* or cleaned slate theory. Naturally our image of ourselves and the world around us influences our scientific perspective as evident in the discussion of intelligence. Recently I read an article in a medical journal which stated that the level of intelligence depends upon the functioning of the brain, and further that brain functions are dependent upon the social environment. The article continued to say that, in order to raise human intelligence to the same level, society must undergo a Marxist restructuring.

CHAPTER EIGHT
Eros as Invalid

L et us now turn our attention from the historical back ground of psychopathy to the condition as it appears and as we encounter it. An understanding of the phenomenon, whether from a psychological, philosophical, or religious perspective, can enable both doctor and layman to alleviate the suffering of the psychopath and of their environment. However, more importantly, an appreciation for psychopathy can help each of us to reduce the damage we do to our own psychopathic side. Finally confronting and dealing with psychopathy gives us a fuller appreciation for what it means to be human. Psychopathy is a borderland of human nature, a border which must be reconnoitered in order to comprehend what characterizes our human geography.

From an historical perspective we can appreciate that there are different kinds of psychopathies which nevertheless manifest a degree of uniformity. Psychopathy is not only something which can be separated into component parts. In keeping with this uniformity and multiplicity, I will speak of primary and secondary symptoms much as psychopathologists refer to schizophrenias. With schizophrenia, as well, we find this admixture of uniformity and multiplicity which is best comprehended through a delineation of primary and secondary symptoms. When I speak of primary symptoms, I mean those symptoms which occur in all cases of psychopathy; secondary symptoms are those which characterize the various types of psychopathy.

As I have said before, we all have *lacunae*, empty places or steppes in our psychic landscape which are our psychopathic sides. However it would be pointless to label all human beings psychopathic. Psychiatrists who have dealt with psychopathy have a particular kind of individual in mind. While they may be different, they still have something in common: primary symptoms. I will describe five such symptoms.

First is the *inability to love*, the lack of eros in the widest sense of the word. I have already spoken of what I mean by eros. Psychopaths can pretend to love or to be in love, frequently fooling those around them with a performance. The murderer I mentioned earlier had a relationship with a woman and went through the motions of being in love with her. He was a gallant suitor, bringing her presents, and talking about the beauty of her lovely brown eyes. He was courteous, expressed sympathy for her and her problems, would inquire about her mother's welfare and about her job. An outsider might well have believed that this was a loving man. However the hollowness of his act is reflected in the following story. While he was in prison, he got into an argument with one of the guards, and the girl friend's name came up. The murderer became furious and shouted that he did not want to have anything more to do with the silly woman; she had never meant anything to him anyway. From that moment on the relationship was over, leaving no noticeable traces with the man. The woman had been taken in by empty gestures.

I would like to make a parenthetical observation to prevent a possible confusion of feeling and love. Although Jung himself wrote little on psychopathy, I am approaching the phenomenon from the perspective of Jungian psychology and should mention the role which typology plays. According to Jung people relate to themselves and their environment on the basis of four functions: thinking, intuition, sensation, and feeling. We experience the world through these four functions with or without eros. We can relate to the world through thinking; by dealing with things through logical categories. It is also possible to experience on the basis of intuition; unsystematically anticipating the connections of things in and around us. The world can also be an "aesthetic" experience for us; relationship through inner and outer sense impressions, images, and colors. Or we can react on the basis of feeling. We feel comfortable or uncomfortable in the company of another person; something in or around us gives rise to a pleasant or an unpleasant atmosphere.

A sensation type is affected by the color of a woman's skirt. A feeling type is depressed and irritable in the same woman's presence. An intuitive suspects that the woman has just criticized him to a mutual friend, while a thinking type considers why it is that the woman blushed slightly on seeing him. He thinks to himself, "She was just talking to my friend, therefore something must have happened in their exchange which made her uneasy. She probably said something critical about me." Neither thinking, sensation, intuition, nor feeling is the expression of a deeper relationship to the woman. She is just perceived and taken note of in an indifferent fashion.

What I am trying to say is that love—eros—may be expressed in and through any and all of the functions, often in unexpected ways. Orthodox Jews use a game called *pilul*, a subtle brain twister, to express their love for God. Love was expressed through thought, through highly complicated, sometimes playful theological arguments and counter-arguments. The scholastics did much the same thing during the Middle Ages. While we might think it bizarre to discuss how many angels could fit on the head of a pin, for the scholastics this pointless, apparently meaningless activity signified the purest intellectual relationship to God.

Regarding a person as being capable of love simply because he or she is a feeling type could have tragic consequences. Mistaking feeling for love is to overlook the fact that relationship is much more than just emotion or perceiving on the basis of feeling, yet it is a mistake easily made. We all know feeling types without a developed eros: they are pleasant and friendly, pat you on the back, and are enjoyable to be with. When they leave, the relationship goes with them. Again and again we confuse feelings with eros. It would probably be interesting to explore the question as to whether or not this were so for other times and cultures.

In our culture eros is enthroned by the cult of interpersonal relations and by the importance given to so-called communication. We revere eros when we caution parents always to be loving and kind to their children. Freud revered eros, whom he saw primarily in sexuality, by creating a vast sexual (read erotic) mythology. Of course our contemporary reverence is the worship of a misunderstood god. Frequently we limit Eros to interpersonal relations and then only to confuse him with feelings. The result is that many psychotherapists believe in all earnestness that the sum total of the world's problems stems from humanity's inability to express feelings, as if expressing feelings could not lead to assault and murder.

Eros is also a force, a power which binds elements of the intrapsychic world. When speaking of Eros, we generally perceive him as that which connects us to our environment, with our friends, and as the power which joins husband and wife, parents and children. As an intrapsychic force Eros effects the connection between elements in our psyches, between our complexes. We no longer view the psyche as an indivisible entity, but somewhat like a nation, with an interplay of various groups and forces. Jungian psychology speaks of archetypes, of innate behavioral patterns symbolized by gods, heroes, actors, even comic-book characters. We speak of the Father Archetype, of the

Mother Archetype, of the archetypes of Priest, Warrior, and Merchant. The relations of these archetypes, one to another, can be either good or bad. Just as gods—one representation of the archetypes—are joined or connected by Eros, so are archetypes in the individual psyche. Eros, then, is expressed not only in my relationship to the outer world but also in relationships between elements of my psyche.

Especially in dreams we have an opportunity to observe how these various parts of our psyche act and react upon one another. One way of looking at dreams is as dramatic plays in which the various figures portray aspects of our psyche. A child which appears in our dreams may relate to a child in waking reality, but it may also relate to the child in us—the Archetype of the Child. In our dreams we observe how this child tries to get along with adults or how he or she acts towards animals or other children. We see in dreams how archetypes relate to one another, whether it is with or without Eros.

Since the archetypes are all connected to each other, it is perhaps not so earth shaking if we occasionally forget a dream or do not consciously deal with it. There are few people who remember as many as one-third of their dreams. The purpose of dreams is not only to remind us of the necessity of dealing with our inner lives. Dreams also provide the stage where archetypes can relate to each other, and how this occurs and the way in which these various relationships develop is of determining significance for the life of our psyche. We could go so far as to regard dreams as a sort of group psychotherapy for archetypes which takes place and has importance whether our humble egos participate in the process or not. One thing is for certain: Eros plays a deciding role in these nightly assignations. It is Eros who mediates between the deities and draws them closer. It is Eros who achieves the relationship of psychic forces.

All this might sound abstract. Let me try to be more concrete. We all suffer from time to time from inner conflicts. Part of us wants one thing, the other part something else: "A house divided against itself." Our child, the child in us, wants to romp and play with no thought of responsibility or duty. Our hero would conquer and rule both outer and inner worlds with daring deeds and heroic forays. These two archetypes, the Child and the Hero, move in conflicting directions. Failing Eros and his relating power, we are pulled first one way, then another, behaving sometimes childishly, sometimes heroically, sometimes judging childish behavior from the heroic perspective, sometimes judging our heroics as a child would. With Eros and his relating quality, both of these "gods" or archetypes respect the other's right to be and take pleasure in the other's being. Both Child and Hero can manifest themselves in us without fear of rejection or rending conflict.

According to what I have just said, it should be possible to recognize psychopathic individuals on the basis of their dreams: a definite lack of Eros' relatedness should be apparent. This is not always the case. Our ability to understand dreams has not progressed to the point where we can recognize the dreamer's psychopathy with any degree of certainty. Nevertheless I would like to relate a dream which to me seems typically psychopathic: the dreamer entered a room full of people and flatulated, causing such an odor that everyone left the room. Another dream has the dreamer standing in a barren landscape. From a distance he sees a child running toward him. An old man comes from the opposite direction. Although their paths cross, neither the man nor the child sees each other, and each goes past or through the other without any sign of recognition or notice. We cannot, it seems to me, speak of a group-therapeutic relationship between the archetypes in these dreams in any sense of the word. What we see is a lack of relationship—in other words, a lack of Eros.

This lack of eros in psychopaths finds expression in difficulties encountered in interpersonal relationships. Rather than eros we frequently find manipulation. Jung said that when Love retreats, Power advances; Power being of signal importance in individuals with psychopathic tendencies. Where eros is lacking, manipulation, control, domination, and intrigue take over. Most researchers have recognized the eros-less quality of psychopathy. Maslow writes, "I found it helpful in understanding psychopaths to assume that they are incapable of a loving identification with others and that for this reason, they can wound, even kill, without scruple, without hate or pleasure, as if they were destroying a harmful animal." He continues, "As far as we can tell, the need to love and be loved has disappeared once and for all." I would like to point out how cautious Maslow is: "I found it helpful. . . to assume; As far as we can tell . . . ."

There are always therapists who assert that they have been able to establish an excellent rapport with psychopaths. Is this actually the case or are they simply fooling themselves? Or, possibly, are they confusing pity for relationship? My experience has been that therapists who do not rightly know the meaning of relatedness are the very ones who claim relationship with psychopaths. I do not mean to imply that this is always the case. Certainly there are individuals whose own sense of eros is so strong that they can succeed in relating even to psychopaths.

CHAPTER NINE
The Missing Morality

The second primary symptom of psychopathy is the *missing or deficient sense* of morality. I said before that a psychopath is capable not only of speaking about morality but also of defending, even advocating it (remember de Maupassant's Belami?) although attaching little or no significance to it personally. But what is morality really? I find myself in a rather precarious situation when writing about psychopaths and saying that they are deficient in eros and morality, I realize that I can neither clearly describe what I mean by eros nor am I able to define morality. While I am operating with images and terminology which cannot be fully grasped, I will try to point out which aspects of morality are significant for our considerations.

Psychologists working out of Sigmund Freud's model of the psyche regard morality as connected to the Superego, itself the result of an internalization of parental images. For instance a father's "You shouldn't do that" to his child is integrated and speaks through that individual's conscience. Those people in a child's outer world who represent morality become the inner voices advocating morality in the adult. Admittedly this is a simplification of Freudian theories of moral development.

Jungian psychologists regard morality from differing points of view. Some assume that there is no general or common morality but that each archetype has a morality of its own. Aphrodite's "morality" would be different from that of Hermes, the merchant and mediator. An individual's behavior, then, would depend upon the operant archetype. A lover, dominated by Aphrodite, would be subject to principles other than those of the merchant, dominated by the Hermes archetype. A wife, in Hera's image, would adhere to different laws than a partier for whom Bacchus might be the guiding archetype. The notion of archetypal morality roughly corresponds to the contemporary view that universal morality has been supplanted by situational morality, in which one can speak of morality only within a given context. Any moral act depends, at least to some extent, upon the particular situation or upon the archetype which dominates that situation. Despite this fact, is there not some "thing," some oneness, that finds expression in the variety of situationally determined behaviors or moralities? The idea of a general or universal morality is still widespread, particularly among those who adhere to the tenets of the Judeo-Christian or Mohammedan faiths. There must be some psychological significance in the concept of universal morality, or it would not be so prevalent and have such a pervasive influence.

Other Jungian psychologists regard morality as the expression of the divine spark in each of us, as the consistency in our psychic inconsistencies, as our link to the Divine. Morality, in its profound, not its profane sense, would be that which contributes to individuation, the process of Self-realization, of relating to the God or gods in us. While the notion has the ring of truth in it, it is not without certain dangers. Highly immoral acts could be excused in the name of Individuation or Self. This is not only a weak point of Jungian psychology. How many crimes have been committed in the name of God? How much evil is perpetrated for the sake of our numerous secular deities like Development, Growth, and Creativity? A man runs off with another woman, deserts his family in order to "find himself" or to "do his own thing." For the sake of her "creativity" a mother leaves her children alone night after night while she attends consciousness-raising workshops and classes on "Being a Better Parent." To be sure we can say that in such cases Self, God, creativity, and such terms have been misconstrued or misunderstood. At the same time it is not simply coincidental that so much that is evil and ugly is done in the name of God, Self, or modern-day counterparts.

Can the Self, can this focal and center-point of our psyche, our divine spark, be immoral? I have pointed out that one of the primary symptoms of psychopathy is a lack of morality. Others agree with me on this score. The Self, that divine spark in us, has to do with the meaning of our existence, a meaning we obtain by realizing the Self. Since apparently there are individuals lacking in all morality, it would not be possible for such individuals to be "saved," if you will, even to approximate a sense of meaning for their lives. They would be, in a word, "damned," a somewhat disturbing thought. It would perhaps be less disturbing to assume the existence of an immoral Self, to assume that the Self in psychopaths contains no morality. That being so, psychopaths would not individuate in a moral sense, Self-realization would not evoke a sense of morals, and their sense of Self would be an immoral one. It rapidly becomes apparent how dealing with psychopathy raises fundamental questions and takes us to the outer reaches of human existence.

I suspect that morality is not so much a question of the Self or even of the various archetypes but one of eros. Morality is the ego's attempt to "get a handle" on eros. The ego, that part of our psyche which attempts to maintain consistency in the inner and outer forces which affect us, tries to systematize eros so that it may be applied in any situation. Morality is the ego's heroic attempt to find rules for the relationship of archetypes among themselves, for our relationships to our fellow humans, and for our relationships to our environment as a whole. The systematizing and the rules are to insure the highest possible degree of peace and harmony. Although heroic, the search for morality on the part of the ego is doomed to some extent to failure, since any morality is replete with contradictions. Unless eros is directly involved, all our attempts to live rightly and lovingly will be unsatisfactory and will appear stiff and unnatural. The ego definitely has more to do with morality than the Self, for Self stands above morals much as God who created a world that is anything but moral, who sends rain to fall on the just and on the unjust, who is Lord of moral and psychopathic human beings, and stands above His creation.

Regardless of how we experience them, eros and morality are somewhat contradictory. Moralists are often not loving, and moral acts often have little to do with eros. Nevertheless it would be wrong to reject or wax indignant toward morality. We cannot rely on Eros. He is a completely unreliable god: sometimes present, sometimes absent. He will not be held or tied down. He does not respond to our volition. Even the most loving of individuals has moments when he cannot love. Perhaps it is for this reason that the ego turns to morality as an ersatz for those times when Eros is nowhere to be found. Love is the first commandment of Christianity, but it is not something which lends itself to commanding. When Eros is absent, the individual wishing to emulate Eros-like behavior has no choice but to attempt to establish a system of values and rules for moral behavior to which one can adhere. It should not be surprising that such rules will be found wanting, since Eros does not allow himself to be ruled.

I do not mean to give the impression that each individual constructs his or her own individual moral system. This is definitely not so. To construct a system which begins even to approximate eros is not only extremely difficult but also requires generations of concerted effort and cooperation with others. Most people are not capable of establishing their own, optimal moral code and humbly have recourse to the code which they are offered by society. Too often we hear caveats concerning collective rules and regulations and overlook the fact that the individual is frequently fortunate to be able simply to adopt a differentiated moral system. Not everyone composes symphonies and not everyone is able to "compose" a moral code. To follow the analogy a step further, we might say that just as most of us sing the songs that are already written, it is advantageous for the majority of human beings to accept the general, existing system of morals.

An average person is in touch with eros from time to time. One's actions are guided by Eros now and again but not consistently. Experiencing eros is not something the ego easily forgets and which it tries to evoke through a code of behavior and morality.

Many psychopaths, possibly the majority, adapt readily. They function well as husbands or wives, as professionals, and in other roles, especially as they grow older and become somewhat mellow. They accept the variety of roles given by society and play them without any real, personal involvement. We must be careful to differentiate here, however. Even an individual who has experienced Eros, who out of a real sense of longing for the return of this most capricious of gods, employs morality as a temporary replacement and plays a role. We cannot live without playing roles. There is a tendency to reject the role-playing that society offers. Jungian psychologists often speak of the *persona*, a mask of which they are rather distrustful. Often in therapy they try to break down the *persona* believing that the analysand is obligated to reject such roles in order to be truly oneself, to be creative and free. The matter is not so simple. No matter how loving we are, no matter how well developed our sense of eros might be, we usually have to express eros within the confines of given roles. In a way it is similar to language. We use particular patterns of speech to express ourselves, generally those which we learned as a child or had occasion to learn thoroughly at a later date. We do not invent our own language.

Another way is to see the world as a stage. Everyone plays a role: beggar, king, warrior, merchant, shepherdess, or whore. Through these roles we express what is particular to each of us as individuals. One of society's tasks is to offer as many and as highly differentiated roles as possible. However playing a role is no indication of psychopathy. Admittedly psychopaths play these roles rather well, but for them they really are only roles, simply masks. The average person's *personas*, their way of presenting themselves, is never totally empty. Perhaps it falls short of completely expressing their being, but it has a certain significance, a certain warmth, and content. It leads to complications, to development, to movement. The psychopath's role-playing is just that, playing, without eros and with little or no morality.

Let me take the example of a teacher. As a teacher he plays the role of teacher. He adopts certain patterns of behavior which are characteristic for teachers. As an individual who now and again has been touched by eros, he expresses through his role his love for his pupils; or else morality, that ersatz-eros, dictates what loving behavior as a teacher would be. If the teacher is a psychopath, he dresses, acts, and talks like a teacher, but it is all a game: neither love nor morality finds expression in his behavior.

In summary the lack of morality in psychopaths results from a lack of eros. Psychopaths can intellectually comprehend morality, can even imitate moral behavior, but morality has no meaning for them; it does not represent eros. This being the case, do psychopaths experience any inhibitions, do they have any taboos? Do they recoil from incest or from consuming their own excrement? Let us take the example of incest, which is common among individuals with psychopathic personalities. Incest for them is not the emotional experience which sometimes occurs between a brother and sister seized by an archetypal passion. Incest does take place between parents and children where none of the parties involved are psychopaths, but it is a powerful, moving, shocking, sinful experience, full of sinister significance. Psychopathic incest is something else entirely; it is not out of the ordinary, just another incident. A psychopathic father, for example, might seduce or rape his daughter, not because he is particularly attracted to her, but simply because his wife is

---

Editor's Note: Hitler, along with being a vegetarian, was known for his coprophilia.

gone, and he is too lazy to go to the effort of trying to find another woman. Similar behavior has been observed in those suffering from brain damage as a result of chronic alcohol abuse.

I had the following experience with a colleague whom I later believed to be a psychopath. A partially eaten apple lay on the floor of a restroom. This colleague asked, "Would you believe that it wouldn't bother me to eat that apple?" I said I did not believe him, whereupon he picked it up and ate it without a sign of revulsion. As near as I can tell, psychopaths do not show the customary disgust for excrement. Some have even told of winning bets that they could eat shit with no difficulty.

CHAPTER TEN
Lack of Psychic Development

The third primary symptom of psychopathy is the *absence of any psychic development* which is used as the basis for diagnosis. Although it is highly practical and easily recognizable, as a symptom it is troubling and a source of controversy. One can be acquainted with a psychopath for a number of years, and he or she does not seem to change. One can work with a psychopath therapeutically or analytically without having a sense of his process. One can be married to a psychopath, and nothing develops, nothing moves or changes. At best we observe a pseudo-development by way of adaptation to external situations or by taking on different roles.

This symptom often finds expression in dreams. Psychopaths' dreams seem to change but little over a period of years. The same thing is said again and again, in the same fashion, without the least indication of inner development. Psychopaths souls' seems static. They, their relationships, and their connections with their environment are always the same. They only grow old, becoming quieter as if they were somehow burned out, causing less damage than in their younger years. A multiple murderer becomes a peaceful gardener. The man who consumed the love and fortune of countless women turns into a boring, stay-at-home husband. Nothing changes with psychopaths; at most they grow tired. An optimist might interject, "Yes, but quietness is still a change for the better!" True, when one considers the suffering psychopaths cause, but we cannot really speak of change or development. It is a question of a gradual decrease in psychic energy, in *libido*. Should aging psychopaths for some reason or other obtain more energy, they would be just as harmful, just as sinister as they were in their younger days. It is not surprising that many psychiatrists have the impression that psychopathy is basically a sexual problem, a problem of sexual *libido*, for psychopathic tendencies decrease with age just as does the sexual *libido*.

The view that little or no development takes place with psychopaths is, as already mentioned, the subject of much debate. Such a thing cannot be. It flies in the face of the tenets of any kind of humanistic psychology, contradicting the humanistic view of human nature. It is contrary to the belief in equality and particularly to the idea of progress. Not to develop would make life meaningless, shaking us to our roots. Whether we like it or not, there are such individuals, psychopaths—and this is something we cannot and should not deny. It does not matter whether the phenomenon fits into our view of things, but what we do with it. Shakespeare wrote in his play *Hamlet*, "There are more things in heaven and earth than are dreamed of in your philosophy." We must include the shocking, horrifying aspects of life among these "more things," not only the positive and pleasant. Certainly it is shocking to realize that there are human beings who are not capable of developing or progressing, who lack a quality which to us seems an essential part of being human.

The lack of growth and of development is, like the lack of morality, the result of a weak or deficient sense of eros; without eros there is no development. Many mythologies portray the new, the growing, the developing as a child, as do our dreams. A child can represent new possibilities, new potential. However a child results from an erotic encounter; an encounter with Eros brings the child. Mythologically, then, the new, the potential, and the child have to do with eros. An individual who is not "erotically" drawn or attracted to something, be it other human beings, an area of knowledge, art, or whatever, has no chance for development. Seen metaphorically, an individual has to be "married" to something, the *hierosgamos* of Rex and Regina* must take place, or there is no psychic process.

What about the saints who led the lives of hermits? They too are guided by Eros, although not eros in connection with other individuals or fields of study, but by eros toward God or through eros to the Self, to that center-point of the soul, that divine spark. Wherever development can be observed, there is eros, either

---

*Editor's Note: This refers to the alchemical sacred marriage which was part of the mysteries of the transformation of the Medieval and Renaissance alchemists in their *opus*.

intra-psychically or connecting us to something outside of ourselves.

Related to the lack of development in psychopaths is their fear of initiation rituals, rites which symbolize the transition from one phase of life to another. A transition is made from one ruling archetype to another, an archetypal changing of the guard with a pomp and ceremony that adds meaning and intensity to the process. There are initiation rituals when a child becomes an adult; others specifically represent a boy's coming into manhood. Still others deal with the transition from single to married life. We study such rituals among so-called primitive, tribal peoples with great interest, from the puberty ceremonies of the Plains Indians to the marriage celebrations of Papua, New Guinea, rituals that we all experience but seldom recognize as such. Confirmation in the Catholic Church bears characteristics of an initiation rite: children are instructed in the catechism, initiated into the religious knowledge of adults and following confirmation, may participate in Mass. Military service, particularly basic training, is often experienced as an exit from puberty rite. The minority who refuse service in the armed forces do so for different reasons: some are pacifists, some refuse for religious reasons, some are simply lazy, and others do so as a rejection of initiation. Some of this latter group are psychopaths, especially in Switzerland where universal conscription is a long-standing tradition. They are men who, incapable of experiencing psychological development, look upon any ritual which formalizes such development with fear and rejection. Not only do they refuse military service, but they also would rather not be confirmed and prefer "small weddings" with just the "immediate family." Rejection of these societal rites of passage is often seen as an expression of originality and a questioning of conventional mores. Actually it is not the conventional being questioned, but rather the ritual of development, the archetypal changing of the guard. For such individuals conventional symbols of psychological development are an abomination. One might say that they have a phobia of development.

CHAPTER ELEVEN
Background Depression and Fear

The fourth primary symptom of psychopathy is what we call *background depression*. Like the lack of psychological development, this symptom too, is a controversial one. For a long time it was believed that psychopaths could not experience sadness. In fact one of the characteristics of psychopaths was said to be their inability to grieve. Their grief is the grief of the invalid. Furthermore it often has delusional qualities: a feeling of despair, the feeling that everyone is against them. We find a similar feeling of mistrustful grief in those who are deaf. Deaf persons are subject to occasional despair as they do not exactly understand what is happening and what others say. Psychopaths are isolated to a much greater degree; their sense of eros, not their sense of hearing, is impaired. Somehow they feel that they lack a quality that moves and guides other human beings, which accounts for their understandably chronic sadness as well as their chronic mistrustfulness.

Chronic background depression is not exclusively symptomatic of psychopathy. We can observe chronic depression as the core of many non-psychopathic individuals' being or at least of their pathology. I would estimate that at least one-fifth of all analysands possess such a core. I prefer to speak of background depression and despair rather than common depression in the case of psychopaths. There are many varieties of depression for which we find corresponding images in mythology. When we hear the term depression, most of us think of the saturnine variety. Saturn was originally a fertility god whose character changed with the passage of time. During the Middle Ages Saturn represented a cold, heavy, melancholic condition, a sense of tiredness, leadness. The Renaissance frequently portrayed images of saturnine depressions: in one, a sad, tired dog lies at the feet of the god, giving the whole a heavy, hopeless atmosphere. Yet saturnine depression is but one of the possible depressive moods and should not be confused with chronic depression.

Nordic mythology appears to express what I mean by psychopathic depression, but care must be taken: the tribes which created the mythology may well have regarded their tales differently than does our modern-day perspective. Nordic mythology best approximates the uncanny experience of sadness which is the lot of the psychopath. The Nordic gods must all die; they all expect the final battle and their own destruction at the hand of the Fenris wolf and Loki's minions. The roots of the world-tree are being slowly gnawed away, and the end is a foregone conclusion. They expect to fight, they will fight, but they know the outcome of the battle in advance. This mythological image—one of inevitable destruction and nihilism—is like the background depression that accompanies psychopaths throughout their lives. Completely different from saturnine depression, it is not manifested in a melancholic apathy and a few tears. There is nothing Romantic or poetic in this form of depression. Some scholars feel that the new creation which is to follow the *Goetterdaemmerung* was the central element in the mythology and not the eschatological "twilight of the gods." If this is indeed so, the mythology acquires a meaning, a hopefulness, and a sense of growth which is otherwise missing.

This background depression, as I have chosen to call it, frequently results in suicides of a nature which appear inexplicable to an outside observer. It may even happen that the individual's life just seems to be taking on some semblance of order when with no warning, suicide occurs. Where Eros is absent, where there is no growth, no psychological development, there is no meaning and no reason for living. We also find a tendency among psychopaths towards so-called social suicide. Most psychopaths adapt well to society.* They are often successful in achieving high social standing only to destroy everything they have achieved through a thoughtless act or provocative behavior. I should emphasize here, too, that social suicide is not exclusively a symptom of psychopathy, it can also result from a neurotic condition.

---

*Here is where I disagree with the mainstream psychiatric view of psychopaths as primarily criminals.

The fifth primary symptom of psychopathy is *chronic background fear*. Psychopaths do not trust the world. Not knowing Eros, they are unable to see him in other individuals except, perhaps, abstractly. Even behavior which is clearly eros-directed seems suspect to them: "What is behind it?" they think to themselves. The background fear differs from neurotic anxiety. Psychopaths' fear is seldom the groundless fear of a claustrophobic in a small room where there is really nothing to fear. Even in situations of actual danger they experiences less fear than the average human being. They realistically evaluate each situation without projecting neurotic fantasies upon the actual danger. In the final analysis, however, the psychopaths are always afraid of everything and everyone. They are always mistrustful, an attitude resulting in unexpected outbreaks of rage and hate, and occasionally, in abstruse thinking.

CHAPTER TWELVE
Sexuality and Religion in Psychopaths

If a lack or deficiency of eros is the core of the psycho-pathic condition, what is the state of sexuality, an area which popularly is viewed as most closely linked with the winged god? Since eros *is* weak or missing altogether in psychopathy, sexuality is not seen as the ultimate expression of an intense, intimate relation-ship between two people. On the other hand it is not subject to neurotic complications which, in the final analysis, result from erotic difficulties. Eros is not lack-ing among neurotics, but it can involve them in severe inner conflicts, inhibitions, and confusions. Actually eros is not the cause of such conflicts but rather morality—the ersatz-eros—with all its inherent contra-dictions.

We notice that sexuality in psychopaths appears less compli-cated and problematic than in so-called normal individuals. Uncomplicated, yes, but also impersonal and unloving, a primary indication of a lack of eros. The physical act, sexuality as a biological phenomenon, presents the psychopath with no difficulties and may even be pro-nounced. In like manner, psychopaths have little difficulty with sexual perversions, being able to express themselves variously—homosexual, heterosexual, or whatever. However regarding sexuality as anything but a physical phenomenon is problematic for them. The symbolic potential of sexuality for expressing everything from a deep and intimate relationship with another human being to numinous, religious feelings is lost on them. Sexuality is simply there, to be used as one would breathe air or drink water. If psychic health were defined as freedom from inhibitions, complications, or compulsions, and freedom from all scruples, psychopaths would be prime candidates. It is this freedom which makes psychopathic sexuality so attractive for others, particularly those acutely aware of the complications, inhibitions, and contradictory nature of their own sexuality.

What about religion? Can psychopaths have religious beliefs? Can they, phrased somewhat naively, trust in the Divine? The answer must be an emphatic, "Yes!" The Self, the divine human spark, is just as recognizable in psychopaths as in any other individuals, an affirmation which is understandable from the perspective of Christian theology. God in his omnipotence can touch any one of His creatures. Not even the most crippled psychic invalid, not even a human being totally lacking in eros is different in this regard. That such individuals can manifest a sense of religious experience continually puzzles us, bringing us to the limits of our human understanding and to an experience of the numinous.

CHAPTER THIRTEEN
Secondary Symptoms of Psychopathy

S econdary symptoms of psychopathy are those which, though not found in every psychopath, character-ize the various types of the disorder. The list is not intended to be complete but to serve the reader as a basis for observation and discrimination. This will en-able the reader to recognize not only who is and who is not a psychopath, but, also and above, all one's own psychopathic traits and tendencies.

An important secondary symptom of psychopathy is the *absence of guilt feelings*. You might ask why I do not include the lack of guilt feelings with the primary symptoms, or how there can be guilt in the absence of morality. However it has been my experience that there actually are psychopaths who experience guilt, albeit guilt of a particular and peculiar nature. Generally speaking psychopaths live in an environment struc-tured by some kind of moral principles, some sense of eros. This results in psychopaths feeling that some-thing is not quite in order, that the way they act is not quite up to par. For them the environment is alien. Incapable of understanding or relating to those around them, they notice that their motivation is different from that of others. They feel alone, misunderstood, and rejected. Frequently they reject themselves as well. They have a sense of condemnation. They know they act improperly but do not understand why. Many psychopaths have the impression that they are always in the wrong, that they can never do anything right, that they are always guilty. Why, they do not know. The therapist must take care neither to confuse this variety of guilt feelings with the guilt which results from moral conflict nor to believe that the presence of guilt indicates the existence of a moral code.

I said that guilt feelings, or the lack of them, is a secondary symptom, though not all psychopaths suffer from this chronic sense of guilt. One also finds the reverse phenomenon—namely, that rather than assume that everything they do is basically wrong, some psychopaths categorically blame everything on others. Psychopaths are not so different from "normal" human beings in this regard: some tend to relate in a differentiated fashion to life and its experiences while others oversimplify everything.

A further secondary symptom is the *absence of any real understanding or insight*. Like the lack of guilt feelings, the absence of insight has often been regarded as characteristic of psychopathy and hence considered a primary symptom. When I speak of lack of insight, I mean that someone may well be capable of intellectually grasping and understanding problems, but that such insight in no wise bears fruit. It is often assumed that psychopaths never learn from their experiences. I view the situation somewhat differently. Certain recidivistic criminals do appear to learn nothing from past experience, with or without intellectual insight. Socially adapted psychopaths claim to understand their difficulties—for example those in their marriage—but their insights are for naught. Psychopaths, whether they are socially adapted or not, live in a different world so to speak, than we do. You might say that they operate on the basis of a different set of coordinates. Many apparent insights which bring no corresponding consequences in their wake are solely the result of external pressure. The environment forces categories and values upon these individuals which result in "insights." Let me cite an example.

A socially maladapted psychopath, a seventeen year-old girl, was committed to an institution for observation following repeated arrests for theft. She was told that she would be under observation for four to six months, and then it would be determined what could best be done for her. She was given to understand that her wishes would be respected and would be the determining factor. Two weeks later she ran away, was caught by the police after five days, ran away three weeks later, was again caught, and so forth and so on. Every time she returned to the detention center, she admitted the folly of her behavior. "There is really no reason for me to run away just because I don't like it here. I'll only get caught, and every time I do run away, I just have to stay here longer. I'm really dumb. I'll just have to stick it out and see what develops." She was not really expressing an insight but merely saying what she knew people wanted to hear. Her actual experience and insight were much different and went something like this: "Running away is exciting, a real change. First off I have to find some way of getting by, spending the night with guys I pick up and experiencing all kinds of interesting things. It is a thrilling feeling to know that the police are after me. When I get caught I spend the night in a police station which also has its good points. Then I'm taken back to detention, and the lectures begin. My teacher gets really mad, but I don't like her anyway. The more I run away, the more fun I have. It doesn't matter to me when they finish their 'observation;' they'll just stick me in an apprenticeship or something. Then I won't have any real reason to run off and knock around the country, and besides the police won't look for me anymore."

That was how the girl told her side of the story on an occasion when she was being open and honest. I should also mention her feelings and attitude toward her environment, something she was unable to express but which were approximately as follows: "I am somehow different from other people. No one likes me, and everyone else seems to live by different principles than I do. I feel better when the situation is clear-cut, in other words, when I am locked up and know that I am being held against my will. Then people are against me, and I can be against them. Being in a situation where people care about me is uncanny. I really don't understand why these people go to so much trouble for me. I would rather fight than have this kind of sentimental acceptance."

Those who know psychopaths well realize that what is regarded as the absence of meaningful insights is, in reality, a misunderstanding on the part of therapists. The insights are not meaningful, because psychopaths experience in a completely different manner than we expect. Occasionally there are cases where, despite rapport between therapist and patient, insights which are understandable in the context of the patient's experience have no further consequence. Only then can we, perhaps, speak of the lack of any real insight.

Another secondary symptom, important for everyone who deals with psychopaths, is their *ability to evoke pity;* the same kind of pity we feel toward invalids or experience for helpless and sick children. How can one help but pity these people, particularly when one senses the background depression and air of despair? They seem completely helpless, lost in a world where they do not belong. Again and again they try to adjust and to cope, in a fashion that always falls a bit shy of the mark. They are the eternal strangers, arousing in each of us a longing to help, a feeling which we experience with helpless human beings. Often this pity creates difficulties, and many is the person who falls prey to it. We often try to be kind to these "poor" people, and they are "poor" people—our pity is justifiable. However the problem is that psychopaths readily manipulate those around them through just such pity. Women are often victimized: mothering instincts are aroused, or the Archetype of the Nurse is constellated. They want to protect and care for the poor, sick thing and understandably so, for psychopaths strike protective chords and speak to the desire to help and heal. Those who have to deal with psychopaths readily succumb to savior fantasies. Confronted by a phenomenon which simply should not be, which somehow must be changed, they set out to save these individuals.

I should not neglect to mention *charm*, another secondary symptom. Decidedly charming many psychopaths have the facility to flatter and please with grace and elegance. Because eros does not clutter their relationships, they can dig into their bag of tricks without any inhibitions or scruples. They know, whether consciously or unconsciously, what pleases and flatters. Since love and morality do not get in their way, they often succeed in utterly bewitching those around them. It must be admitted that a psychopath's company, usually not unpleasant, is even restful and relaxing. As a rule they make no moral demands on us; in fact, they make no demands whatsoever. Every real relationship is tiring; relationship requires an effort. Actually people who are guided in their activity by Eros or the ersatz-eros—morality—are always a little tired. They may well wish to be done with morality for a time and to speak and act as the mood strikes them. With psychopaths our own moral scruples disappear. This is not to say that we necessarily become immoral, but rather that we get the feeling that morality is not of major importance, obviating the need always to appear moral. We can laugh and gossip about others at will and at least indulge in immoral fantasies. However a psychopath's company is as quickly forgotten as it is leisurely and relaxing. It is not so much that the experience leaves a sense of emptiness behind, but that it is, in itself, somehow empty. It is not something which is missed.

Always on guard against possible misunderstanding, I should say that the reverse does not hold true, simply because we enjoy being with someone, we should not conclude that that individual is psychopathic. Some people have a talent for putting others at ease, for making them feel good about themselves. This is a special kind of eros; a warmth, a depth, something quite different from the psychopath.

Parenthetically I might add that psychopaths arouse envy. To a certain extent we would all like to be like them, unencumbered by morality with its scruples and tensions, a morality which often lies at the root of our neuroses. Also it seems that psychopaths age more slowly, their faces remaining enviously smooth, free of the wrinkles and furrows impressed by conflict and worry—like the face of Dorian Gray in Oscar Wilde's novel. Female psychopaths often seem girlish in their appearance well into old age.

But back to the secondary symptoms. I would consider *asocial or criminal behavior* a secondary symptom. While every psychopath suffers from or manifests the five primary symptoms, any particular psychopath can, but need not, manifest one or more secondary symptoms. This is significant insofar as asocial behavior is concerned: a psychopath can be asocial.

I would go so far as to say that asocial, criminal behavior is relatively rare among psychopaths. Understandably, but regrettably, literature on the subject concentrates upon this aspect. Many criminal psychopaths have been institutionalized or imprisoned and hence lend themselves to study and observation. Socially adapted psychopaths are not as readily observable. At best we get to know them on a personal basis. Therapists, psychiatrists, and psychologists have little professional contact with them, because they have little motivation to seek out therapy. Unfortunately numerous criminal or asocial individuals are diagnosed psychopaths but are not. Because of this I purposely cited two cases of asocial behavior where the diagnosis psychopathy was incorrect: the first case was of a member of a subculture and the second of the neglected girl. We must differentiate between psychopathy and neglect even if there are certain common symptoms. Neglect is a social-neurotic disturbance of development; psychopathy is not.

Given the proper circumstances and conditions, most psychopaths can turn criminal. They are more likely than other individuals to risk coming into conflict with the law. Socially adapted psychopaths do not avoid criminal activities, because they are basically opposed to them, but because they want to adapt. At any time a psychopathic businessman might go to the outermost limit of what is permitted. He may even risk transgressing those limits from time to time and might get caught at it. Here we are not dealing with social behavior as a secondary symptom but with behavior which results from assuming a certain risk.

Among psychopathic criminals—by no means are all criminals psychopaths—we find harmless, weak individuals on the one hand, and dangerous, aggressive ones on the other. The harmless ones experience their chronic condition in terms of being caught up in an ongoing guerrilla struggle against their so-called normal environment, a chronic conflict resulting actually from their own particular form of invalidism—lack of eros, morality, etc. Society plays according to rules which, despite hypocrisy and mendacity, are basically informed by eros and morality. Thus to psychopathic people the rules of society are foreign, even laughable. They do not see the point of the rules, so they can break them easily. Such individuals lack the strength and rigor to adapt to a world with its alien rules and regulations. They are comparable, for example, to a foreigner who has lived in the United States for twenty years without learning a word of English, who yet complains about everything and everyone.

The brutal psychopaths are considerably more dangerous than the weak ones. Somehow nature has endowed them with a goodly measure of aggression. All of us are more or less aggressive, more or less able to stand up for ourselves. Someone who is not granted the experience of eros and is also extremely aggressive is bound to have major difficulties. The world is foreign to psychopaths, and as foreigners they cannot trust those around them as they all harbor animosity toward them. *Homo homini lupus.* Under certain conditions the combination of pronounced aggressiveness and a despairing sense of alienation in an unfamiliar world can result in brutality, murder, and rape. Some of these aggressive psychopaths succeed in channeling their aggressiveness in socially acceptable directions where they are respected and feared, and for this very reason, economically successful. Their families and business partners are the ones who have to suffer from their reckless brutality.

We can also see some forms of *boredom* as secondary symptoms of psychopathy. A life with little or no eros or morality can readily turn into a dreary, monotonous affair. Psychopathic individuals can call upon only a limited amount of inner reserves. If they are lucky, Eros does put in occasional appearances, if only brief ones, in the form of some interest like gardening, handicrafts, or painting. When Eros absents himself altogether, the vacuum is filled with meaningless or destructive activity. Such individuals move compulsively, restlessly from one activity to another. Part of the attraction in driving a car—naturally, not the only one—is that a certain psychopathic vacuum becomes filled. Racing along a turnpike at eighty miles an hour and frightening the law-abiding drivers by cutting in close in front of them can be an enjoyable way to pass time. Some people find a similar fascination in travel, visiting foreign countries more to fill an inner emptiness through exposure to ever new stimuli than out of interest in other peoples and cultures. Blaise Pascal in his *Pensees* talks about *divertissements* (diversions). Also symbolic significance can be seen in the drive toward warmth in the direction of the southern sun that many tourists exhibit. One compensates almost compulsively for inner coldness by external warmth; one lights up inner darkness by Florida sunshine. We seek the geographic south to escape the polar ice cap of our psyche. Worth mentioning at this point is the "jet-set," a source of Walter Mitty fantasies and Madison Avenue illusions. The term conjures up images of a social class which is at home everywhere: breakfast in Zürich, supper in New York, as familiar with London as with Rio de Janeiro. We imagine svelte, suave, and elegant couples who transcend national and social limitations, apparently with roots everywhere but in reality with no roots at all.

To experience eros is to be rooted. Eros binds to the specific and the particular, to family, to social class, culture, people, language, and nation. Lacking eros one has no connection, one levitates above the world, one has no roots. We are all, as I will repeatedly insist, partially psychopaths. Perhaps this is the reason we are so easily hooked by jet-set fantasies and illusions.

Social-climbing must also be counted with the secondary symptoms. De Maupassant's hero, Belami, provides a precise psychological portrait of the phenomenon. All of Belami's energy is concentrated on attaining the uppermost rung of the social ladder and finding recognition in that position regardless of the cost to people or morals. The tragedy of psychopaths,

127

their loneliness and despair, is revealed in such social climbing. As outsiders among human beings, invalids lacking an essential something, they can only compensate for their differentness with social success. Their suffering, their depression, and their unloved and unloving qualities are mitigated to some extent through social acceptance. Basically asocial, unconnected to the society in which they live, psychopaths see themselves confirmed by the determining strata of that very society. In addition to the recognition they achieve, psychopaths obtain a sense of power as well. Those who cannot relate to others on an eros level can do so on a power level.

CHAPTER FOURTEEN
Psychopaths and Compensation

When I speak of compensation in this context, I refer to balancing a psychic defect through special effort—i.e., people who have a poor sense of time look at their watches continuously and are overly punctual. Dealing with compensated psychopaths moves us away from patients in a mental institution and closer to the person on the street; closer to you and me.

Extremes are rare in psychology. Practically speaking there is no such thing as a "pure" psychopath. By the same token there are few individuals who do not manifest at least some psychopathic traits, the large majority of the human race lying somewhere between psychopathy at one end of the spectrum and sainthood on the other. Saints, those in whose company Eros is always to be found, have no need for the ersatz-eros—morality; and "pure" psychopaths, lacking the experience of eros, lack its stand-in as well. For those between the two poles, the stronger the sense of eros, the weaker the need for morality; the weaker the sense of eros, the greater the moral need. Here I will be talking about those who are dangerously close to the psychopathic end of the spectrum, those with only a hesitant sense of eros, where their representative—morality—has difficulty filling the gaps.

Individuals approaching the psychopathic extreme are not totally wanting in morality, but they do sense a weakness, an awareness that something is missing, which frightens them. They also suspect that their love is not all that it could or should be. In order to adapt they begin to compensate for these deficiencies becoming morally rigid. Rather than, or perhaps in order to prevent falling into a state of total moral and ethical apathy, they turn compulsively moralistic, championing moral causes for themselves and for others more fanatically than anyone else. These are the people who are always talking about principles, always concerned about "the principle of the master." They get so lost in principles that they never notice the need for a little milk of human kindness by way of balance. Compensated psychopaths tend to seek out occupations where those with whom they work will help to maintain a moral rigidity, occupations where a strict morality is the order of the day. Therefore we would not be surprised to find large numbers of compensated psychopaths in the so-called helping professions: teaching, psychiatry, the ministry, social work, and the like. It is, for example, difficult for a clergyman to live a completely immoral life. His profession makes him the moral authority, a representative of Eros in the highest sense of the word, whose task it is to convince others that these values are the ultimate ones. His professional role enables him to shore up his own weak morality and his almost absent sense of eros.

Since compensated psychopaths cannot depend upon eros, their egos work out a moral system which is fool-proof in any and every situation. The result, as paradoxical as it may seem, is usually a well-developed morality with an emphasis upon the ego's role but woefully lacking in love. Compensated psychopaths continually and at all costs uphold moral conventions, fanatically defending their moral systems. Were they to relax the hold on their moral code, the entire structure might well collapse like a house of cards, revealing their psychopathic nature. It is rather like cooking, a poor cook sticks assiduously to the recipe, while a gifted one can change this and that according to a momentary whim.

Compensated psychopaths have played significant parts in society and in history. The more psychopathic compensated psychopaths are—in other words the more they have to compensate—the more sinister they are. All the Nazi functionaries who administered the concentration camps and supervised the destruction of thousands and thousands of human beings; all of Stalin's subordinates who, during the time of the Soviet purges, directed the arrests and deaths of innumerable individuals; all of Mao's minions who so efficiently effected the disappearance of large portions of the Chinese population—certainly all of these people were compensated psychopaths.

I am reminded of Adolf Eichmann (the German Nazi official who as head of the Gestapo's Jewish section was chiefly responsible as the organizer of the "Final Solution"), a man who was relatively conscientious and dependable. Not a devilish monster, he was rather a classic example of a compensated psychopath whose conscientiousness was greater than that of most individuals. He loyally and admirably carried out the "duty" of exterminating his fellow humans, but his very dedication to "duty," expressing his own alienation in this world, vented so heinously his hate toward all human beings who were not like him. The commandant of a concentration camp wrote in his diary at the close of the war: "It is very sad that I can no longer fill my daily quotas in the gas chambers. I have neither enough staff nor enough supplies. Every night I go to bed with a nagging conscience, because I have been unable to do my duty." We can see how conscientious this man was. A classic, compensated psychopath, he had a strong, rigid, "moral" system but not the slightest sense of eros. The morality which sought to replace the missing eros turned into a farce becoming a caricature.

Compensated psychopaths are probably the most reliable supporters of a dictatorial regime, the emphasis being upon "compensated." A dictator could not function surrounded only with "pure" psychopaths—his regime would achieve nothing, eventually collapsing in utter chaos. A dictator's subordinates have to be conscientious and obedient—in a word, *compensated* psychopaths.

Summing up we can say that the symptoms of compensated psychopaths are the following: moral rigidity, moralism, compulsive attention to duty and order, pedantic adherence to any and all regulations, and exaggerated conscientiousness.

The warning I gave in connection with "pure" psychopaths bears repeating as far as compensated psychopaths are concerned. It is not my intention to place us on one side and the compensated psychopaths on the other. We all have psychopathic sides which we attempt to compensate. My chief concern is that we recognize *how* we compensate our psychopathy, *how* we compensate our *lacunae*, since I am taking it for granted that none of my readers consider themselves one of the saints.

CHAPTER FIFTEEN
Aggression, Shadow, and Eros
The Miracle of Why Psychopaths
Do Not Rule the World

In the preceding discussion of the primary, second-ary, and compensated symptoms of psychopaths, I spoke only briefly about aggression. Since many people automatically link psychopathy with aggression, something should be said about the subject if only to avoid misconceptions. Right at the start let us make the distinction between aggression and the core or essence of that element we call the shadow—a distinction Jungians make—but which in most psychological texts is anything but clear. Aggression is the ability to fight, to win, to assert oneself, but it is also the ability to dispose of one's adversary without being troubled by too many scruples. Aggression is not so much the desire to defeat one's opponent, but rather to advance oneself. Lawyers, for example, try to win their cases not to harm the other party, but so that they and their clients may achieve what they want.

As it is defined in Jungian psychology, the shadow consists of several different levels. We define the shadow as those elements, feelings, emotions, ideas, and beliefs with which we cannot identify, which are repressed due to education, culture, or value system. The shadow can be primarily individual or primarily collective—

the former when we are the ones, personally, repressing particular psychic contents, the latter when an entire culture or subculture effects this repression. For instance certain conceptions of sexuality and instinct can be relegated to the shadow. In a particular family anger may be viewed as something so reprehensible that, as children grow older, they will not show anger openly, and it can only exist in the realm of the shadow. Another example is a split between official tolerance of other nationalities or races and racism that privately thrives as a part of our collective shadow.

One might note the shadow is a complex matter comprised of different elements. Because it is a complex, it has as its basis an archetypal core, a potential for behavior with which we have probably been born, which might be designated the murderer or suicidal element, that which is in and of itself destructive. A point which is widely debated is whether or not there is such a thing in human beings. Jungian psychologists assume that human nature includes an archetype which is primarily destructive—Freud's Thanatos instinct, the instinct to destroy and be destroyed. It would be easy to conclude that the shadow with its destructive core and aggressive component is of central importance in the understanding of psychopathy, especially when we regard psychopaths as individuals who commit shocking and aggressive acts. However, remember that we have distinguished between aggression—or the instinct of self-assertion—and the shadow element of psychic destructiveness.

As I stated before we can consider aggression as a quantum, something of which some individuals possess more from the time of earliest childhood. We all know aggressive people who compensate, when eros is absent, with a differentiated moral code. Put somewhat simplistically aggression serves these individuals to move from desiring good to living and asserting what is good. On the other hand psychopaths or compensated psychopaths employ aggression to achieve their own egoistic goals. Compensated psychopaths with a great deal of aggression dominate their classmates, family, or business associates with their harsh and unyielding morality. When, however, there is little aggression present, the story is quite different. Both the individual with some experience of eros and the compensated psychopath have difficulty asserting themselves and in reaching their goals, regardless of what those goals are.

Even that archetypal core of the shadow, what we have called the ultimately destructive elements of murder and suicide, does not really have that much to do with the actual problem of psychopathy. That core we all have and worry about. It shocks us when we see it at work in ourselves and in others, something we can observe on the highways of any country in a suicidal manner of driving; especially evident in youthful motorcycle riders, their reckless disregard for the life and limb of themselves and others, flirting with death, tempting the grim reaper. Although the murderous elements are usually deeper than the suicidal ones, we

ADOLF GUGGENBÜHL-CRAIG

observe them occasionally when a motorist brushes
past a pedestrian in a crosswalk or passes a stopped
school bus. Usually it takes a war to bring out our
"murderer," and then it is dumbfounding how so-called
normal men, neither psychopaths nor compensated
psychopaths, succeed in simultaneously killing their
fellow humans and revolting and disgusting themselves.
Even the vicarious pleasure we all derive from a murder mystery or from the brutality of some films seems
to remind us of our own murderous characteristics.

While the murderous and suicidal aspects may seem
uncanny or even inhuman to us, they are crucial for our
lives because they are linked to the psyche's creative
potential. In his book, *Moses*, Leopold Szondi demonstrates how the truly creative individuals also possess
destructive sides. Szondi introduces his argument with
the case of Moses, whose "case history" begins with the
murder of an Egyptian overseer and ends with his
becoming the father of his nation, leader and lawgiver
in one. One is tempted to conclude that a strong archetypal shadow, what we called the murderous and
suicidal elements, results in a high degree of creativity
when combined with an equally powerful sense of eros.
This same conflict, the conflict between love—for one's
fellow human, for one's environment, for one's psyche—
and a murderous passion for destruction, drives the
individual to the borders of an existential framework.
What the murderer would destroy, eros would renew,
and out of the admixture of the two—destruction and
renewal—comes something creative, comes the Creative.

Though a pronounced Archetypal Shadow is not characteristic of or determining for psychopaths, a shadow without eros, which can wreak considerable havoc, is. Just as certain psychopaths willingly surrender themselves to sexuality in any form, so those who are unequivocally psychopathic sometimes have little hesitation about living out the core of the shadow; the murderer/suicide. The results are often shocking and monstrous; acts which, in truth, occur much less frequently than we are led to believe but which are then pointed out as being typical for psychopaths. In the first place there are few pure psychopaths, and these seldom have particularly strong shadows or Archetypal Shadows. Furthermore the desire to adapt and prevail in the world, even if it is an alien one, usually holds psychopaths in check when it comes to living out their shadows.

Because psychopaths provide particularly fertile ground for the cultivation of our own shadow projections, when we do not pity them, we hate them, seeing in them our own destructive potential. Actually we make into demons those psychopaths who have called attention to themselves through criminal or pseudo-criminal activity. We demonize those who have committed murder and are astounded to discover how harmless they seem when we really see them. Infamous swindlers and cheats appear to be the Devil incarnate to us. We enjoy reading about people who achieve notoriety from their hook-or-by-crook approach to life, who do not even stop short of murder. We see them as instruments of evil and destruction, and all the while they are merely invalids, human beings lacking something essentially human.

Contrary to popular belief there are certain advantages to being a psychopath or compensated psychopath. Many of them have a relatively easy time adapting to society, unencumbered as they are by moral or neurotic scruples. They replace the lack of love or of true relationship with a love of power, something they can achieve without much difficulty owing to the absence of moral or eros-related restraints. Even a compensated psychopath can find room for a justification of unrestrained power seeking within a rigid morality. It is little wonder that psychopaths occupy so many of the top positions in society and rather astonishing that there are not more in such positions.

Let me put it somewhat differently. One of the major problems of any society, of any political or large organization in general, is that of preventing unscrupulous, socially adapted psychopaths from gradually taking over. There are many countries in which the problem is a long way from being solved. There are certain countries whose political organization encourages psychopaths to rise to positions of power, even where only psychopaths can achieve such positions. It is not difficult to imagine in what spirit such nations are ruled. Nazi Germany was a good example. The former U.S.S.R. and all dictatorial forms of government, be they left-wing or right-wing regimes, are certainly to some extent dominated by psychopaths. Stalin was probably a psychopath with a pronounced shadow and a decided power drive. Trotsky, originally his friend, was more of an idealist. But observe—Stalin died of natural causes at a ripe old age; Trotsky was murdered. There seems to be some truth to the expression, "the good die young."

One is inclined to ask how, in a democratic country, we may prevent psychopaths from inveigling their way to the top. The power of the highest administrative positions is so strictly curtailed in Switzerland, for example, that it hardly tempts psychopaths. It seems to me more important that the people be able to see through a psychopath, to see through their own psychopathic side. In most democracies this ability is well enough developed so that a dangerous psychopath is usually detected when he or she appears on the scene.

I am convinced that a democracy whose citizens are incapable of discerning a psychopath will be destroyed by power-hungry demagogues. In Switzerland the resistance towards "great men" and the preference for mediocre political figures would seem to result from an instinctual desire to prevent psychopaths from coming to power. Although there is certainly such a thing as a "great man," many such figures are probably nothing more than unrecognized psychopaths. Think of personages such as Alexander the Great, Genghis Khan, Napoleon, William XI of Germany, and many other more or less esteemed leaders of the past and present. These "great" criminals—and one must include Hitler and Stalin among them—destroyed the lives of

141

millions. Themselves "erotically" stunted, they succeeded in obtaining recognition and power over societies in which they felt shut out; power which was necessary to maintain the illusion that they actually belonged. Happy is the nation which gives such "great" men (and women) short shrift.

CHAPTER SIXTEEN
The Treatment of Psychopaths

Psychopaths rarely come into psychotherapy. When they do, usually they have been forced by external pressures—as for example by the court seeking to clarify questions arising from a criminal proceeding, or when one partner in a marriage is threatened with divorce and goes into therapy to see if anything can be salvaged from the relationship. One can almost guarantee that, if someone comes into psychotherapy believing that they need help, and that with hard work and dedication a way out of their difficulties can be found, then that person is not a psychopath. I have seldom met psychopaths in my practice who were not under some sort of social pressure, although occasionally the background depression and despair leads the psychopath to seek out psychiatric or psychotherapeutic help. These are the times when one can get a little closer to psychopaths, when one can share their despair and can show them that they, too, are human, a part of the creation with a right to a meaningful existence. Work with psychopaths requires of the therapist both a great deal of tolerance and the eros-given ability to be totally unmoralistic. Even with these prerequisites the measure of success will be limited.

Aiming for success, or striving for the healing touch, or to put it another way, the inflation of the analyst is the greatest danger in dealing with psychopaths. Here we reach the limit of our ability to heal, and it is never pleasant to be confronted with our own limitations. We would like to believe that we can help anyone who comes, for whatever reasons, seeking our help. We would like to believe that no symptom, no complaint, no difficulty can withstand our talent, our ability, and our understanding. Here we get caught, as they say, between a rock and a hard place. Since psychopaths understand our weakness, our need to help them against our better judgment, they can use us, manipulating us to the point where we start defending them, writing letters of recommendation for them and the like. To take the situation one step further, we react to psychopaths as we react to all human beings. We feel pity and sympathy, savior fantasies are called forth, our feelings of mothering and fathering are awakened. While all this may be true, at least psychopaths have come into contact with someone who confronts them as honestly as possible, an approach which provides them with some relief if only for the moment.

With compensated psychopaths we often make the mistake of misconstruing their rigid, moralistic attitude as neurotic, as the result of an overdeveloped super-ego, as the expression of an overly restrictive conscience, and as an inability to allow and enjoy anything for themselves. In the interest of relaxing what we perceive as the strictures of a compulsively moral individual, we attempt to dismantle the conscientious structure. We say things like, "Is it really necessary for you to eat supper every day at the stroke of seven o'clock?" Or, "What if you don't feel like cooking or have something else you would rather do? You could always eat at eight or even at nine." We try to get the morally rigid housewife to loosen up a little, to live a little. We do not see that when the compensatory elements of a compensated psychopath are removed, the whole system tends to collapse. In other words if the housewife did not cook supper at seven o'clock every evening come "hell or high water," she would not be able to cook at all; she would not be able to do anything. If the patient clerks in a bank, we might ask him why he does not ease up a little in his compulsive attention to duty, only to receive a postcard from the same man a week later from Rio de Janeiro whence he has absconded with a small fortune in the interests of an extended vacation.

As therapists we have to be certain as to what we are doing before we start dismantling the structures of compensated psychopaths. In this regard it seems important to me to remember that one of the primary symptoms of psychopathy is the lack of development. When we are dealing with psychopaths, it means that from the beginning we should give up any hope for development or any expectations we might have that some kind of inner development on the part of the patient will improve their situation. Rather we should try to help the man or woman to find an external situation in which they will be relatively happy in spite of their psychopathic nature. This is decisive in treating psychopathic teenagers. A girl who earns her living as a prostitute, because she is psychopathic, should not be prevented from plying her trade in the interests of inculcating her with social and moral values. Instead one should try to help her find the best and safest way to be a prostitute so that neither she nor others are harmed. It is a matter of finding the proper environment—if at all possible—for the psychopath in question. To use an historical example, the Vikings set up special groups of particularly aggressive psychopaths—the Berserkers—who were used in battles when "average" soldiers were unable to advance any farther. Of course such a solution is only possible for particularly aggressive, masculine psychopaths and would not be at all applicable for socially adapted individuals.

In a modern, relatively complex society, it should be possible to find a role which psychopaths could fill for the good of the entire society without causing an undue amount of difficulty or harm. We all tend to believe that, in a nascent social structure, such as in pioneer America or during the time of the first settlers in Australia, psychopaths could have constructively contributed to collective goals. I seriously doubt if such were indeed the case. The more primitive and rudimentary the social structure, the greater the amount of eros required of each individual for the proper functioning of the group.

THE TREATMENT OF PSYCHOPATHS

For years, even decades, the attempt has been made to treat psychopaths, to help them and to heal them. Every possible method has been employed: they were dealt with harshly or with understanding; they were locked up in institutions and given intensive attention; therapists tried to identify with them. No matter what was done, if the literature on the subject is to be believed, everything was doomed to failure. Again and again someone would come along claiming to have found some new psychological approach which would help such individuals, and repeatedly it turned out that nothing could be of any help. Various forms of pharmacological therapies were also explored with few if any positive results. Despite a great deal of time, trouble, and energy, the end result was inevitably disappointment.

Many members of the helping professions have developed a sort of therapeutic nihilism, a resignation and despair in connection with psychopathy. There is some danger that therapists and social workers who deal primarily with social adaptation cases may end up working principally with psychopaths, because they are intelligent, arouse sympathy, and demonstrate a certain charm. Should such social workers be disappointed time and again in their attempts to help psychopathic clients, they might well begin to ask themselves whether or not they are in the right profession. If the social worker falls prey to the belief that psychopaths are human beings like any other (human beings who can be helped and healed), they will be severely disappointed, perhaps giving up their profession. It is important for therapists that, when they recognize a client or patient to be a psychopath, they avoid spending too much of their time and energy on him/her, saving it for those cases where their efforts will be effective and helpful.

CHAPTER SEVENTEEN
In Praise of Morality and Good Manners

We know little about the causes of psychopathy. We do know that certain brain trauma can lead to psychopathy-like conditions, an observation which has stimulated considerable research into organic causes. Neurological examination has revealed a significant number of abnormalities in electroencephalograms of psychopaths, a line of investigation which has proven otherwise unfruitful. Part of the problem is that many researchers start from incorrect premises, assuming, as they do, that antisocial or criminal behavior is a sign of psychopathy. I do not share this view, as I hope I have made abundantly clear. Therefore the groups of individuals selected for research seldom include significant numbers of psychopaths.

Psychological research seems also to have met its match in psychopathy, a fact which is not terribly surprising. We are still trying to understand how and why certain individuals are gifted artists, while others are talented musicians, and still others can neither paint nor carry a tune. We do know that a human being may have many talents and abilities, but why some individuals approach the level of genius while others are blathering idiots in the same area is beyond our comprehension.

In Jungian psychology we assume that archetypal forces play a deciding role in our psychic life, that various archetypes affect us and find embodiment in our lives. Aphrodite, the goddess of love, may determine our behavior, or Hermes, the sly and clever trader, or Ares, the warlike and quarrelsome, or one of the Muses. Perhaps our abilities or lack of abilities are related to the meaning or meaninglessness which certain archetypes have in our lives. Still we have no idea why more of one archetype and less of another is constellated in certain individuals. To get to the crux of the matter, we do not know why Eros "neglects" some individuals, and why there are "erotic" invalids.

In the first section I talked about invalids; we are all somehow, somewhere, invalids. Invalidism is a classical, typically human situation which leads to the supposition that there must be an Archetype of the Invalid and a corresponding archetypal response to invalidism. Having begun with a consideration of invalidism in general, I moved to the most serious form of the phenomenon—the invalidism of eros. We all have a particular image of humankind, of what a human being is and how we relate to such beings. Eros, taken in the broadest sense of the word, plays a decisive role in all of these images. Some researchers maintain that human beings are born as a *tabula rasa*; that love—eros—is something we learn from our environment: "I love because I have been loved." Yet no matter how Eros comes to be, the ability to love is one of the deciding characteristics of our humanity. Most of the religions of the world concern themselves with eros, with love in general, and encourage it, demand it, transfigure it, describe it, and so forth and so on. One of the most important teachings of Christianity is, "Love your neighbor as yourself," and one of the hymns proclaims, "God is love, again I say, God is love."

Psychopathy brings us face to face with a form of invalidism which jeopardizes our image of humankind, confronting us with individuals who, in extreme cases, are incapable of love. Admittedly such extreme cases, what we have called "pure" psychopaths, are rare. By and large psychopaths are individuals who can love only to a limited extent, experiencing the touch of Eros only now and again. Possibly they experience eros only in connection with their stamp collection, but never where other human beings are concerned. Eros may touch many things for us or a very few; what he touches blossoms, what he leaves untouched withers. Should, for example, he touch your possessions, then all of your attention would be devoted to furniture, carpets, and house while those who live in the house go wanting. Or, perhaps, the emphasis might be reversed. A woman might have a strong sense of eros and be loving and caring toward her children, her husband, her family and friends while having no relationship whatsoever toward her household, letting everything go to ruin. She is a psychopath as far as material possessions are concerned.

Psychopathy forces us to ask these shocking questions, "How does it happen that many individuals lack what gives life meaning? Why are there those whose invalidism is in an area which is ultimately human? Why do some people have no sense of eros at all or only to a limited extent?" In psychopathy then, at least as it is portrayed in this work, we are dealing with the ultimate form of invalidism, the standard against which we measure our ability to deal with our own invalidism as well as the invalidism of others. We can, at least theoretically, deny it by simply holding to the assumption that there is no such thing as psychopathy or invalidism. We might say, "Sure, there are those who have a limited ability to love or even none whatsoever, but that is because something went wrong somewhere along the line: their parents were unloving, society was repressive, their nutritional balance was incorrect during their growing years, or possibly some infectious disease has impaired something. Basically, however, there should be no such thing as psychopathy!" But there *is* such a thing . . . and we do not know why.

Even nature leaves a psychopathic impression: life in the animal world, the lives of the various animal and plant species seem to occur under the aegis of mutual coexistence but not of eros. Parenthetically it might be noted that humanity's relationship to nature for the past several centuries has been markedly psychopathic without the slightest semblance of eros. As far as nature goes, we are all a bit psychopathic.

Because we have to live with our own psychopathy and that of those around us, it is essential that we at least be in a position to recognize it as a phenomenon.

We need to be able to recognize that we have friends or relatives who are so lacking in eros, so psychopathic that we can expect nothing from them. We should try to make their—and our own—lives more tolerable by reining in our proselytizing in the name of love, and by giving up our attempts to change *them* to fit *our* expectations. For those in the helping professions, it is important to know that some clients cannot be changed, that there are those from whom we can expect no improvement, but whose lot we can improve only through external measures. It is also necessary to recognize our own erotic invalidism with which we are continually confronted in the course of our everyday activities. We ought not to expect too much from ourselves, either. If it seems that our psychopathy manifests itself in our inability to love those outside our immediate family, we should not waste our energies in the attempt to maintain a large circle of friends, despite all of the fashionable prattle about the importance of interpersonal relationships.

We always experience the psychopathic side of others within the framework of intimate, close relationships. Instead of simply accepting the phenomenon much as we would accept that it rains from time to time, we allow ourselves to be disappointed again and again, much like those adults who demand the same kind of loving interest that they received as children from their parents. Human beings are the way they are and not the way we wish they would be.

What does this most complex of all invalidisms have to offer us by way of psychological significance? For one thing it dispels any illusions of Paradise. People seem to believe that, in the long run, we can create a Shangri-la if only the system, our organization, our approach to education, or something else is changed. In this way we will succeed in bringing a happy, healthy world into being. Psychopathy, the invalidism of eros, thrusts us back into reality, forces us to look at the naiveté of our image of humanity and progress, an image which has a strong influence in modern psychology as well. We cannot conjure up Eros like a rabbit out of a hat in a sideshow attraction. This is a fact of life. And if he only shows himself occasionally, if at all, we have to accept this, too. The complete or partial lack of eros makes us humble, expelling the *hubris* of our expectations of Paradise. We are continually confronted with the "monster" in us and about us. Quite possibly the task of Eros is to help us to accept our own monstrosity and that of others along with that of psychopaths.

With our newly won—I am tempted to say "philosophical" humility—we return to values that have long been trodden underfoot. I am speaking about morality, both the individual and the collective varieties, even the attendant rules of etiquette and manners. Where there is eros, there need be no morality or regulation of deportment. We all agree on this point. Since most of us rarely experience eros directly and some of us never, we ought to value his humble intermediary,

morality, more highly, no matter how rigid and un-pleasant it may seem to us. It is easy to poke fun at the limitations, one-sidedness, and relativity of morality's maxims, but it is quite another matter to live without conventional mores, no matter how compensatory. We should be grateful for morality's crutch. Without it life would be Hell for most of us; we would be wolves in human clothing.

We should also be grateful for that aspect of morality we call good manners. We cannot always be kind and loving to those around us. We are all invalids as far as Eros is concerned, something to which we must ad-just. Having conventional forms of deportment allows us at least to hint at the presence of Eros or to behave so that others might believe Eros is present. Naturally when I am introduced to someone and say, "I'm pleased to know you," it is only a conventional figure of speech. However what the expression implies is that if Eros were present, I really would be happy to have made a new acquaintance. It is a crutch allowing me to seem "erotic" even if Eros has absented himself for the mo-ment.

Decrying good manners and morality as being hypo-critical is like saying that someone who is missing a leg is hypocritical for wearing a prosthesis. True, the person with only one leg has only one leg, and it might be more honest, after a manner of speaking, for her to hop around on the only leg she has. On the other hand her artificial limb makes it easier for her to move around and may even give those with whom she comes in contact the impression that she has two legs. The better, as they say, is enemy of the good. It would certainly be *better* if all our actions *were* directed by love, but since this will never be the case, any attacks on morality and good manners are dangerous. Destroy them, and we are left not with love but rather with a gaping void. We may not be able to win the battle against disease, but we may have won a sense of our own limitation, our own humility. In this spirit and because of my own, our own, monstrosity, may I humbly proclaim, "Long live morality!"